# NAVIGATING the
# PRINCIPALSHIP

# NAVIGATING the PRINCIPALSHIP

KEY INSIGHTS FOR
NEW AND ASPIRING
SCHOOL LEADERS

**JAMES P.
SPILLANE**

**REBECCA
LOWENHAUPT**

**ASCD** | Alexandria, Virginia USA

1703 N. Beauregard St. • Alexandria, VA 22311-1714 USA
Phone: 800-933-2723 or 703-578-9600 • Fax: 703-575-5400
Website: www.ascd.org • E-mail: member@ascd.org
Author guidelines: www.ascd.org/write

Ronn Nozoe, *Interim CEO and Executive Director*; Stefani Roth, *Publisher*; Genny Ostertag, *Director, Content Acquisitions*; Susan Hills, *Acquisitions Editor*; Julie Houtz, *Director, Book Editing & Production*; Katie Martin, *Editor*; Judi Connelly, *Senior Art Director*; Masie Chong and Mary Duran, *Graphic Designers*; Kelly Marshall, *Interim Director, Production Services*; Cynthia Stock, *Typesetter*; Shajuan Martin, *E-Publishing Specialist*

All web links in this book are correct as of the publication date below but may have become inactive or otherwise modified since that time. If you notice a deactivated or changed link, please e-mail books@ascd.org with the words "Link Update" in the subject line. In your message, please specify the web link, the book title, and the page number on which the link appears.

PAPERBACK ISBN: 978-1-4166-2771-5  ASCD product #118017     n8/19
PDF E-BOOK ISBN: 978-1-4166-2773-9; see Books in Print for other formats.
Quantity discounts are available: e-mail programteam@ascd.org or call 800-933-2723, ext. 5773, or 703-575-5773. For desk copies, go to www.ascd.org/deskcopy.

Library of Congress Control Number:2019943014

28 27 26 25 24 23 22 21 20 19          1 2 3 4 5 6 7 8 9 10 11 12

For Penelope Peterson, a leader and scholar,
who has fundamentally shaped our field, and
for all school principals with the courage to lead.

**JPS & RL**

# NAVIGATING the PRINCIPALSHIP

Acknowledgments ................................................................. ix

1. Stepping into the Principal's Office ............................... 1

2. Bearing Responsibility ...................................................... 23

3. Diverse Stakeholders ........................................................ 37

4. Managing Tasks and Time ............................................... 51

5. Cooperation and Coordination ...................................... 63

6. Sharing Leadership ........................................................... 81

7. Creating a Safe Space ...................................................... 96

A Final Word ........................................................................ 111

Appendix: Study Methods ................................................. 116

References .............................................................................. 118

Index ....................................................................................... 121

About the Authors ............................................................... 125

# ACKNOWLEDGMENTS

Writing in general, and writing a book in particular, is a collective endeavor—collective in several senses. First and foremost, we could not have written this book without the generosity of two cohorts of Chicago principals who shared their journeys of becoming principals by filling out our surveys and engaging in conversation about themselves and their work over several years. We strove to honor their accounts of successes, struggles, and commitment to their work, and we do our best in the pages that follow to use their words to capture and develop the core themes of the book.

This book is only possible because of a wonderfully talented team of interdisciplinary researchers who listened and argued and engaged in the hard work of not only designing a longitudinal research study centered on new principals but also collecting and analyzing these data. We are most grateful to our colleagues in the Principal Policy and Practice Research Study: (in alphabetical order) Lauren Anderson, Kaleen Healey, Megan Hopkins, Allison Kenny, Linda Lee, Leigh Mesler Parise, Michelle Reininger, Matthew Shirrell, Jonathan Sun, Carolyn Swen, and Rongzhen Zhou (www.distributedleadership.org). The dedication, capabilities, and collaborations of these scholars laid the foundation for our book. At the very outset of this endeavor, Dan Lortie gave us wonderful counsel and sage advice that contributed tremendously to our work; we are very grateful.

Research is costly, and without the very generous support of the Spencer Foundation (Grant #200900092), we could never have carried out this program of research. We are most thankful to the Spencer Foundation, not only for their funding but also for their vision of supporting solid social science that generates useful and usable knowledge centered on crucial issues in education. We also appreciate the generosity of Northwestern University's School of Education and Social Policy and Institute for Policy Research for their support for this project. Boston College's Lynch School of Education and Human Development also provided crucial support for our work.

Last, but by no means least, we appreciate the ongoing input from several colleagues, in particular those who read and responded to a full draft of the manuscript: (in alphabetical order) Coleen Coleman, Shelby Cosner, John D'Auria, John DeFlaminis, Diana Guzzi, Eithne Kennedy, Penelope Peterson, Penny Sebring, Jonathan Sun, Jonathan Supovitz, Carolyn Swen, and Allan Walker. In addition, we are grateful for the wisdom of Susan Hills and Katie Martin, whose editorial insights helped shape the work. We also wish to acknowledge our partners and families for their support, always, and input along the way.

Of course, we take responsibility for all opinions and conclusions in what follows, including any errors we may have made.

# 1

# STEPPING INTO THE PRINCIPAL'S OFFICE

All kinds of people become principals. Some bring a decade or two of class-room teaching experience to their new principal position, while others come with just a handful of years. Some are seasoned administrators who have spent a decade or more in various school leadership positions, while others are novices in the world of school administration. Some enter schools they know little about, while others assume the principal position in schools where they have worked for years and know inside out.

Some actively pursue the principal position. Others were coaxed into it by colleagues and family members. Kathy, a 40-something Caucasian mother of three, is an example of the latter. She never imagined she would become a principal, despite having grown up in a family of teachers and principals. As Kathy put it, "The day I graduated from college, my grandmother said to me, 'I know you'll be a principal someday.' And I thought, 'Oh, never!'" When Kathy was a teacher, colleagues encouraged her to pursue a leadership career. The first principal she worked for pushed her to get her administrator license and then supported her internship. Finally, after more than 20 years as an educa-tor and a stint as an assistant principal (AP), Kathy stepped into the position.

Whether those who become principals actively pursue it or were encour-aged by others, as Kathy was, they tend to share two common motivators: a desire for personal fulfillment and a sense of social obligation.

## PERSONAL FULFILLMENT

Alejandro described his path to the principal's office as a series of professional moves in an ongoing search for more challenging work. "Growing up as a kid, I never wanted to be a teacher," Alejandro recalled. Nonetheless, he valued the six or seven years he spent in the classroom. "I really enjoyed myself teaching," Alejandro explained. "Then I started to lose a little desire. It was not so much that I didn't enjoy the kids; [teaching] just wasn't as challenging for me." Taking the assistant principal position in the school where he taught offered Alejandro new opportunities for growth. However, after a few more years, and although he liked that work too, he began to feel dissatisfied all over again. Seeking new challenges that would stimulate him and help him grow, Alejandro took his first principal position at Hoptree Elementary.

Located outside Chicago's city center, Hoptree serves several hundred students in grades pre-K through 6. Nearly all of these students receive free or reduced-price lunches. Most students at the school identify as Hispanic,[1] and almost half of the student body has been identified as English language learners. The neighborhood where Hoptree is located has long been a home to immigrants. European immigrants flocked there in the late 1800s, and a century later, Hispanic immigrants, along with some eastern Europeans, began to move in. Over the first decade of the 21st century, the neighborhood became primarily Hispanic.

Alejandro, a Hispanic man in his 30s, was born and raised in Chicago and spent the first part of his career as a teacher and assistant principal in the district. Shifting neighborhood demographics, entrenched divisions among staff, and the school district's decision to put Hoptree on probation due to poor student performance on state tests meant that as a new principal, Alejandro was facing many challenges. He knew the school district had high expectations for him, and he welcomed that. As he put it, "If I'm not making a difference

---

[1] Throughout this book, we use the term *Hispanic* to honor the language used by the principals whose stories we share and to align with the district's use of the term as a designation for students. However, we acknowledge that the term is problematic, originating in U.S. federal government documents and emphasizing a history of colonization. We recognize that many who might be identified as Hispanic would choose other terms to describe themselves. We refer readers to a detailed discussion of terminology in Suárez-Orozco and Páez (2002).

here—not just based on [the district's] standards but on my standards too—then I shouldn't be here. Quite honestly, I should do something else."

Although Alejandro did not see his new position simply as a stepping-stone, he suspected it would not be his career finale, either. He expressed interest in serving as a district administrator someday, perhaps an associate superintendent with responsibility for curriculum and instruction, as that would allow him to have a broader impact on more than one school. Alejandro explained that, for him, the bottom line was having challenging work. "I want to be here as long as I feel challenged," Alejandro explained, "but I'm open to going on to a different challenge—not in any set time period, but when the opportunity arises."

For educators like Alejandro, becoming a principal is the logical next step once the work of assistant principal no longer provides sufficient challenge. It is a way to find stimulation and keep growing professionally and personally. Oscar, a new principal at Tulip Elementary, voiced a similar enthusiasm for learning, and this commitment figured prominently in his pursuit of the principal's office. A Hispanic man in his mid-40s, Oscar had spent two decades as an educator, 10 of them as a classroom teacher, when he realized he was ready for a new challenge. "I was looking for an opportunity" Oscar explained. "I had been an AP for six years already. I felt [becoming a principal] was my next step; there was nothing else for me to learn."

A few weeks before he began his first year as principal at Tulip, Oscar shared,

I've always been the person who likes challenges and likes to keep progressing and learning new things. Right now, I feel that I'm there, I'm learning some things that I didn't know. I feel that when I was an AP, I got to a certain limit. But now, as a principal, there are a lot of new issues for me to learn about, and I like learning.

## SOCIAL OBLIGATION

It's common for educators to step into the principal position because they are seeking opportunities for professional growth and self-actualization. But intertwined with this somewhat individualistic and personal focus is a sense of social or moral obligation—to society in general, and to its more vulnerable members in particular.

Oscar took his first principal position at Tulip, a large elementary school serving a high percentage of Hispanic students. After working as a teacher and administrator for over a decade, being principal at Tulip helped address Oscar's thirst for new challenges. At the same time, he purposefully sought out a school in a Hispanic community where he might become a community leader and a role model. "There were very few models up there for students, and we have a large population of Hispanics," Oscar explained. "I think it is important that our students see some people who are like them in leadership positions. That was something that motivated me to become a principal." For him, the principal position offered the possibility for both personal fulfillment and social service—motivations that are closely intertwined for him.

Kathy's first principal position was at Nyssa Elementary, a small magnet school on Chicago's North Side that serves a diverse student population drawn from neighborhoods across the city. She had worked there for numerous years as an assistant principal before making the move to the principal's office. She, too, was motivated by a sense of social obligation. As Kathy put it, "We are present for the kids and for their families. My vision is that we provide resources and provide support for our children who are going through difficult times, and their families as well." For Kathy, becoming a principal was about obligation, a desire to help others who are less fortunate.[2] Serving Nyssa's students was her first obligation, but she was also committed to helping families.

A sense of responsibility for and obligation to others was also central to Nelson's decision to be a principal. A 30-something African American who was himself a graduate of the school district, Nelson wanted to work in one of the lowest-performing schools to fulfill this sense of obligation to serve others. He explained, "I want to feel like I'm being of use. It's how I get motivated, because students are behind their potential. That's the only way I could get

---

[2] This is what John Goodlad (1990) refers to as "moral obligation," a sense of social responsibility to work on the behalf of others. While Goodlad's work focuses on this sense of obligation among teachers, our work shows that this same commitment carries over into the principalship.

really, really motivated about it." A former football player, Nelson started his education career as a teacher and coach. Through coaching, he recognized his talent for motivating and influencing others and decided to pursue a career in leadership. "I'm a people person," Nelson explained, "and, as I go back over my coaching, I guess I was a player's coach. My players would always want to run through a brick wall for me."

After stints as an assistant principal, Nelson was confident that he was ready for his first principalship at Birch, a large, low-performing elementary school with a primarily African American student population. Birch was the sort of school Nelson had been searching for, one where he could fulfill his sense of social obligation. He explained that he had been raised by parents who provided regular access to parks, museums, and a host of other out-of-school activities. Compared to his own experiences, Birch's students seemed to have very little. The chance to create opportunities for them that they had been denied by virtue of circumstance was a prime motivator for Nelson. As he put it, "It's really on me. I get to get out there and do what I feel needs to be done."[3]

Becoming a principal is a way for many educators to continue working directly with children and deepen the commitment to service that drew them to the profession in the first place. Alejandro explained that becoming a principal was a way to have a bigger impact while still being able to work directly with students. "As a young teacher, I figured I could save the world," Nelson remembered. He explained, "I have to be able to help kids, and that's what keeps me going—seeing the look on their faces when they're learning and knowing that I had a lot to do with that." Kathy described a similar commitment and a similar sense of reward. "Being the daughter of a teacher, I grew up surrounded by teachers, and I'm very, very comfortable in this environment," she said. "I spent a year at central office about 10 or 11 years ago, and I hated

---

[3] Some principals' characterizations of their social obligation seem to reveal a form of "deficit thinking," which does not take into account the assets, or funds of knowledge, students bring from home (Moll, Amanti, Neff, & Gonzalez, 1992; Valencia, 2010). Others may caution against jumping too quickly to charges of deficit thinking, noting that the ways people speak about and with children from their own backgrounds can be easily misinterpreted (Delpit, 2006; Ladson-Billings, 2009). We defer from passing judgment on such matters and choose instead to highlight these principals' sense of moral commitment to improving the lives of others.

that. I hated working in a cubicle. I will always be with kids. It's the best part of this job. I can't ever imagine moving beyond the school level to do something that didn't involve kids."

## CHALLENGING CIRCUMSTANCES

Becoming a principal offers plenty of opportunities for educators seeking new challenges—and this is often especially the case for those who choose to work in an urban environment. While today's classrooms may look similar in many respects to classrooms 100 years ago, the circumstances in which schools operate have changed in several important respects. Significantly, over the past quarter century or so, state and federal policies have reshaped the circumstances in which teachers and school administrators work.[4] Standards and high-stakes accountability tied to student assessment results have become staples in the daily work of both teachers and administrators. Policymakers and the public writ large hold schools accountable based on their performance on a few key metrics—chief among them student achievement and attendance. The charter school movement has introduced an additional element of competition. Principals must navigate these changing and challenging circumstances as they transition into their new role.

### Performance Metrics

Just prior to Nelson's first school year as principal, the district informed Birch that student and teacher attendance rates, test scores, and graduation rates all needed to increase. Nelson took the job knowing that these measures would be the means through which he would ultimately prove his value to district administrators. Metrics were also a core concern for Kathy, even though she became principal at a relatively high-performing school under no threat of district probation. As she explained at the time, "The district expects me to take the school to the next level. They expect the reading scores to be higher."

---

[4] The shifting context of education policy over the last 20 years has been the subject of much analysis and writing. See Mehta (2013) or Spillane (2009) for a detailed accounting of how education reforms have reshaped the work of educators in U.S. public schools.

Government policies increasingly hold school principals and their staff accountable for their performance, usually on a handful of performance metrics. Most principals are well aware of the need to attend to performance metrics. While student achievement in core school subjects tends to be their chief concern, they also focus on two other metrics: student attendance and teacher attendance. Although some feel pressure to raise scores primarily from the district and sometimes the state, others also feel accountable to communities, parents, and themselves. Regardless of where the pressure comes from, principals feel a sense of urgency about getting the scores up. Principals who work in particularly challenging circumstances can feel helpless. Nelson reported feeling like it would take a miracle to improve the performance metrics at his school, comparing his situation to "being on the *Titanic* and we're heading toward the iceberg. I'm spinning the wheel and trying to keep us from hitting it."

Principals may be aware of the limitations of mandated performance metrics, but they know they cannot ignore them. Most are of two minds about these measures of and guideposts for academic development. For example, although Oscar recognized the use of student test scores in driving improvement and as an indicator of progress, he lamented the heavy focus on them. "We're creating human beings. They need to be prepared and to be given exposure to the arts, the humanities, and all that," Oscar said. "Sometimes we just have to focus so much on making sure that we have the scores for reading and math that we limit students' exposure to other things."

When he took the principal position at Tulip Elementary, Oscar promised himself that once students' scores in the core tested school subjects improved, he would expand the curriculum so that students could experience a broader array of subjects—ones he believed to be essential for cultivating "good human beings, good citizens." Of course, Oscar's ambitions depended on more than just the efforts of Tulip's staff and would take time. A principal who tables a proposed action until after certain performance metrics are met might find it takes years to hit those marks, long after the current students have moved on. Yet faced with the very real accountability pressures of testing, Oscar and other principals who are similarly motivated by social obligation maintain their commitment to do more than just teach to the test; they strive to fulfill a duty to care for students in a more holistic way.

## Competition

Today's principals cannot take student enrollments for granted. Competition from charter, magnet, and private schools means principals must ensure families opt for their school and are satisfied with the services it provides. In some respects, this increases the sense of urgency surrounding improvement on performance metrics, but it also means acknowledging that families are often looking at much more than student achievement data when selecting a school. Oscar explained, "You want to have a place where parents and children want to be." Principals like Oscar know that the competition for students requires considering factors beyond how well the school does in terms of the handful of metrics that district administrators use to evaluate a school. Parents have a broader repertoire of things they consider in choosing a school for their children, such as school culture and community.

As a principal in a high-achieving magnet school that has a high profile with the public at large, Kathy definitely felt the press of competition. Because parents actively opt to send their children to Nyssa, they constantly challenged Kathy to provide particular services tailored for their children. And then there are parents who have the means to be demanding in all aspects of society, so they feel that they should be able to be demanding in school too. Some parents expected Kathy to have her staff tutor their children one on one after school to ensure the children's competitiveness in the high school placement process. For principals like Kathy, competition also comes from outside the system—from neighboring charter schools, private schools, and the threat of school closure. It's not uncommon to lose children to nearby competitor schools that are not necessarily any better in terms of student performance but have "great marketing." Principals must manage these complex competing pressures if they are to maintain and grow enrollments.

## Policy Churn

While standards, high-stakes accountability tied to student assessment, and competition may be staples in the policy environment, instability is everywhere. Policy churn is a constant, with district and state policymakers regularly changing their minds and enacting new policies and regulations on everything from evaluating teacher performance to budgeting. In part, this is because policymakers are always trying to figure out how best to incentivize and support instructional improvement. It also reflects the reality that district administrative regimes are striving to make their mark.

As one principal described it, keeping up with constant changes in the policy environment feels like "surfing without a surfboard." Responsible for compliance with a vast array of demands, principals must learn about and work with teachers to implement new testing policies, curriculum standards, teacher evaluation approaches, and other reforms on an ongoing basis. And often, once they learn how to address one set of policy requirements, the requirements change. Being a principal means adapting constantly.

## Growing Poverty

Circumstances are further complicated by rising and increasingly concentrated poverty among families of school-age children. High poverty combined with decreasing government funding for many social service programs create a need-based vacuum in which school systems are left, often by default, to provide basic services such as meals, clothing, and mental and physical health services.[5] These environmental circumstances create significant challenges for school leaders in their attempts to address the diverse educational needs of their students.

## MANAGING DILEMMAS

Addressing these and several other challenges means principals must work to define problems and craft solutions to match their commitments and values. Nelson, well aware that metrics like student attendance and performance could make or break him and his school, had to figure out why student attendance at Birch was not where it ought to be. There are several ways to define

---

[5] See Orfield, Ee, Frankenberg, and Siegel-Hawley (2016), which highlights the ways in which poverty, race, and segregation combine to influence schools and school systems.

a problem like lagging attendance, and doing so involves more than just gathering data and crunching numbers. It may have to do with how students are treated by school staff, or perhaps it's related to students being bored by classroom academic work or feeling disrespected by their teacher or student peers. Then again, attendance problems may have nothing to do with the school but rather with circumstances beyond the schoolyard. Perhaps students don't feel safe coming from and going to school due to gang violence or other neighborhood circumstances. Perhaps the problem of student attendance might be more accurately defined in terms of some combination of these circumstances.

Defining problems is difficult work because problems are not tangible things that lurk under the floorboards of the schoolhouse, awaiting discovery by a new principal. Problems are social constructions, built on the subjective interpretations of those who encounter them. How problems are defined is critical. As Mark Moore (1976) reminds us, different problem definitions can lead to distinctly different ways of resolving problems, and the consequences are immense.[6] Facing an ongoing string of challenges, principals construct solutions according to their definitions of the problems through a process of diagnosis (see Chapter 5). But they do not do this alone. They engage staff and other stakeholders in problem solving in an attempt to do the work in a way that will enable change in everyday practice in their schools. And there is no shortage of problems for principals to solve.

Although problem definition and problem solving are at the heart of being a principal, it's important to pay special attention to a particular type of problem—what Larry Cuban (2001) refers to as "wicked problems" or "dilemmas" (p. 10). The challenges that both Nelson and Oscar encountered with performance metrics went beyond defining and solving problems of attendance or student performance. Both principals were torn between focusing on performance metrics as measured in terms of student achievement in a couple of school subjects and making room for much broader ambitions for student learning. As you will see in the pages ahead, both Nelson and Oscar embraced more comprehensive, holistic notions about student development.

---

[6] For more discussion of the implications of problem definition, see Moore (1976).

What both Oscar and Nelson were presented with was a dilemma—in Cuban's definition, one of those "messy, complicated, and conflict-filled situations that require undesirable choices between competing, highly prized values that cannot be simultaneously or fully satisfied" (2001, p. 10). To confront a dilemma is to face alternative solution pathways that are roughly equally desirable, either of which requires some compromise among closely held values. Choosing one of these alternatives over the other is difficult, if not impossible.

Theorists (and we include ourselves among them) might argue that principals should resist state- and district-mandated performance metrics that limit the scope of a broader educational mission, but principals do not always have the luxury of theorizing. As Nelson explained, "I can't sit back and be an armchair quarterback; I'm actually on the field." Student achievement metrics can't be ignored, because they have real consequences for the school, for a principal's job security, and for students themselves, whose achievement on state tests will very likely matter to their futures. But could someone like Nelson also be expected to ignore a deep commitment to creating meaningful learning opportunities for students?

Dilemmas aren't like ordinary problems, which can be solved with technical solutions. Because dilemmas derive from a clash of values that are roughly equally compelling and in constant conflict, they can't really be solved at all. But dilemmas can be managed through a process of ongoing negotiation and renegotiation. Learning to cope with dilemmas and to accept them as a continuing feature of the work is a key skill for all new principals—and it's a particular focus of this book.

We are not the first to emphasize the importance of recognizing and managing dilemmas. Scholars have documented the centrality of managing dilemmas in the education sector, from Magdalene Lampert's (1985) work on classroom teaching practice to Larry Cuban's (2001) work on educators and administrators. Michael Lipsky (2010), focusing on the public sector more broadly, documents how managing dilemmas is central to various forms of public service work ranging from teaching to social work.[7] Dilemmas are part

---

[7] Read Lipsky (2010) for a discussion of how other public services manage dilemmas similar to those that factor in education.

and parcel of life in general and life in schools in particular, where competing demands, the unpredictability of human interaction, and unanswerable
issues confront teachers and principals on a regular basis. For these reasons,
it's essential for new principals to learn to cope with and manage dilemmas
rather than burn themselves out trying to "solve" that which is insolvable.

In our usage, *managing* (i.e., coping with) dilemmas is in no way pejora-
tive. It hints at *no* mediocrity or failure. It's life, and as David Cohen (2011)
and Michael Lipsky (2010) so brilliantly remind us, it's especially life when
one is a practitioner of human improvement and working in the public sector.
Principals experience myriad challenges—some of which involve definable
and solvable problems, and some of which are rooted in ongoing dilemmas
that they must learn to manage. New principals must also learn to distinguish
between ordinary, solvable problems and the larger dilemmas they must manage rather than solve. This is no easy task, and from our perspective, managing dilemmas is a key benchmark of managing to lead.

This critique of the education field and other public sectors has been
referred to in various ways by shrewd observers. The push to identify action-
able solutions and generate productive output is what Ball (2003) terms
"performativity" and Majone (1989) calls "decisionism."[8] Similarly, Lampert
(1985) refers to the pressures that teachers face in playing the role of technical-
production managers. She highlights the importance of sitting with uncer-
tainty and acknowledging the messy complications of dilemmas. In distinct
ways, these scholars critique the field for embracing easy solutions at the risk
of ignoring the many unsolvable conflicts inherent in the educational enter-
prise. Cuban (2001) reminds us that focusing on solutions for hastily defined
problems can often lead to more problems. While recognizing that problems
are everywhere and problem solving is an important aspect of the work, we
seek to draw attention to those wicked problems that cannot be resolved—
dilemmas—and the importance of managing these dilemmas on the job.

---

[8] See Ball (2003) and Majone (1989) for more detail about the pressure to resolve problems and
produce action.

## NAVIGATING DIFFERENT CROSSINGS

All new principals encounter challenging circumstances that give rise to problems and dilemmas for them to manage, but their initial encounters with these circumstances do differ in a key respect. Some principals are homegrown, native to the schools where they assume the principalship, having worked there often in various positions for several years. In contrast, others are strangers, outsiders to the buildings where they take their first principal position. These two different "crossings" pose some unique navigational challenges.

Some principals, like Kathy, assume the principal position in schools where they have worked for several years. Others, like Nelson, assume the principal position in schools where they are unfamiliar with the school culture and practices. Crossings are difficult, and the circumstances vary widely. Some new principals inherit an entire staff when they transition into the position, while others get to hire most or even all their staff as they transition. To complicate matters further, some have planned their transition into the principal position, whereas for others, the transition is unplanned.[9] Some are hired to disrupt, whereas others are hired to maintain.

### Inside Crossings

Upon taking the assistant principal position at Nyssa, Kathy began working closely with the principal on all aspects of leadership. Even though she never planned on being a principal, over the course of several years as assistant principal, she was groomed to succeed the principal with whom she worked closely. She reported feeling fortunate that she had the opportunity to learn from her predecessor, who provided her with many opportunities to experience the leadership role. Kathy explained, "In my role as assistant principal, I was blessed that I was not stuck with the dirty work." Encouraged by her predecessor, Kathy pursued the principal opening at Nyssa and, with support from the staff and community, stepped into the position as part of a purposeful succession plan.

---

[9] For further discussion of principal succession, see Spillane and Lee (2014) and Lee (2015).

One advantage Kathy had coming from inside was that she had the trust of the Nyssa staff and parents. Her reputation at Nyssa was such that the local school council, although it advertised the position and received applicants, decided not to interview anyone else for the job. They wanted Kathy. "I didn't interview," she explained, smiling. "Being hired was beautiful, such a wonderful testament to the community's trust in me. They chose to just offer me the position." Laughing, Kathy added, "It was, other than the birth of my children, the greatest day of my life."

Not only did Kathy enjoy the support of her local board, but she also had the advantage of knowing Nyssa and the families the school served; she was well acquainted with staff members and the school's interpersonal dynamics—all knowledge that any principal hired from the outside would have needed months of time and effort to figure out. Kathy said, "I know the people, I know our instructional programs, I know the areas where we have made great strides, and I want to continue in that direction. I know the areas that we need to focus on." Three months into her tenure, Kathy offered an early assessment of her staff as happy and supportive of her as principal: "The feedback has all been very positive. They will say to me things like, 'You know, I really appreciate how you keep us informed.'"

Janice, a Caucasian woman in her mid-40s who has spent almost her entire education career at one school, Poplar Elementary, was also encouraged to apply for her initial administrative position by her principal. She explained,

> I was still getting my administrative certification, and the principal waited for me to finish. She went a whole year without an assistant principal. She said, "I really want to put you in this position." So that's how I got out of the classroom. I was truly expecting to be in the classroom more years, but the position happened to open up here.

By the time Janice took over as principal at Poplar, which is located in a low-income neighborhood and enrolls mostly Hispanic students, she had been at the school for well over a decade as both a teacher and administrator. "I knew the climate and the culture of the school," Janice explained. "I knew the people. I knew what the school's vision was, what we were working toward, what people were dedicated to accomplishing. I was already part of that, so I didn't have to learn or figure out the culture of the school." From their first days in the principalship, Kathy and Janice knew the lay of the land, how things worked, and the various stakeholders they would have to satisfy.

While crossing from the inside has its advantages when assuming the principalship, it also brings its own set of challenges. As an insider, it can be difficult to shift staff expectations to enact change. Janice experienced this as an assistant principal who moved into the principal position:

> Because you're kind of associated with a previous principal, they see you as one and the same. The biggest transition that I had to make here at this school was getting the staff to realize that, even though I was part of the former administration, I would make changes and things would be different.

Janice explained that she admired the previous principal, with whom she had worked closely, but her priorities were distinct, something she needed to convey to the staff who expected her efforts to support the previous principal's priorities.

Kathy also struggled to shift staff expectations of her as she crossed into the principal position. As Nyssa's assistant principal, she worked hard to be always available for staff and build open, trusting relationships with them. As a new principal, though, she felt the need to set additional boundaries in order to protect her time and her work as the leader. She explained that with her history of maintaining an open door policy, staff "are used to coming in this door whenever they want. I'm concerned about that challenge, and I'm thinking about putting in limits so I can get things done." Although both Kathy and Janice could draw on deep knowledge of the school and strong relationships, their crossings came with the challenge of establishing themselves, their agendas, and their relationships in new ways.

## Outside Crossings

Others take the helm of schools they know relatively little about through direct experience, bringing an outsider's perspective to both their new school and its staff. These principals experience an even steeper learning curve as they gather information and build new relationships. While they bring expertise from the outside to their new position, they need time to figure out how things work in their new schools and what stakeholders expect of them and the school. As Oscar put it in the early days of his principalship, "I've only been here for a couple of weeks. I'm still learning about people, about what's in place, about programs that might or might not work." For Oscar, looking, listening, and learning were key first steps in building relationships with staff and other stakeholders he didn't yet know.

For Alejandro, navigating new relationships is one of the most daunting aspects of the job. He explained it this way:

> I think coming into a new building where I didn't know anybody, the hardest part is just not knowing people's strengths or areas they need to improve. Not only the unknowns on a professional level—about them as instructors, about knowing what they're really good at. But also knowing how sincere people are and how open and trusting they are with you.

As the dynamics among staff came into view, Alejandro began to see the need to influence social interactions as the first step in pursing his agenda: "If I could unite the faculty, that would be a huge accomplishment. I mean, it amazes me that everybody loves working here, yet there's this subculture where nobody likes each other." Alejandro laughed before continuing, "I'm going to break that subculture. I have to; otherwise I'm not going to get anything done."

Some aspects of entering the principal position from the outside can make the transition easier. Unlike Kathy and Janice, who both needed to assert their own priorities despite expectations, Alejandro and Oscar benefited from the assumption that they would bring change to their schools. Staff expect new initiatives from newcomers. As Oscar explained,

> They expect me to bring a different kind of school environment to create. It's something that I'm working on. I've had some good comments about how people feel that I am open to their opinions and that I listen.

While Alejandro and Oscar both viewed their initial steps as listening and learning, they also actively sought to align what they heard to the goals they were bringing to their leadership roles.

Regardless of whether principals cross into the position from within or outside the school, they step into complex leadership roles within a complicated and changing environment. Ultimately, they will need to rely on their staff to help them respond to the many demands that various stakeholders have placed on them.

## THE BOOK AND ITS OBJECTIVES

This is a book about practitioners, for practitioners, and based on the accounts of practitioners. By *practitioners,* we mean school principals in particular but also school leaders who might aspire to be a principal. Our audience also includes those who work with school principals, including school system staff, professional development providers, and education policymakers.

In the pages to come, we explore the principalship through the accounts of newcomers to the position. We have endeavored to capture the work of *becoming* and *being* a principal by sharing the experiences of 11 principals as they transitioned to and were socialized into the position over their first few years on the job in Chicago public K–8 schools. We use pseudonyms for both the principals and their schools. However, whenever possible, we use their own words to relate the everyday headaches, heartaches, and successes that new principals typically experience in the early years of the 21st century. In Figure 1, you'll find a brief description of each of these principals, some of whom you have already met. You will glean additional details about each as you move through the book, but the information here will help you distinguish among them.

While the stories of the principals in this book are particular, their experiences are more general. We are confident that the challenges they face mirror the experiences of new principals in many places. Our hope is that by sharing their stories and the dilemmas they managed, we can help others anticipate and manage their own crossings and meet the challenges that come with moving into the principal's office and not only becoming but *being* the principal.

**Figure 1.** Meet the Principals

**Alejandro** became principal at **Hoptree**, a K–8 school, after 10 years of teaching and several years as an assistant principal. Hispanic and in his mid-30s, Alejandro grew up and attended school in Chicago and became an elementary school teacher after college. After various positions in the district, Alejandro felt prepared for his move into leadership. When interviewed, Alejandro frequently referred to the importance of articulating his vision for instruction. He explained his belief that a good principal must be a strong instructional leader who is "willing to either provide the in-house professional development or seek outside resources to make sure that teachers are prepared to do the best job they can." Alejandro was deeply invested in his staff's growth, viewing his Instructional Leadership Team as "the heart and soul of the school."

**George** entered his first principal position at **Buckthorn Elementary**. Caucasian and in his early 30s, he grew up in a family of educators and described himself as driven by a commitment to serve others. He taught for only a few years before training as a principal. When he was a special education teacher, George was inspired by his mentors to pursue the principalship and enrolled in a nontraditional principal preparation program. As a new principal, George was drawn to try strategies that were "out of the box" to accomplish goals related to academic achievement. He was committed to transparency and described his leadership style as laid-back and "laissez-faire," stressing that he had "no problem making mistakes and owning up to those mistakes."

**Janice**, Caucasian and in her early 40s, began her career as a teacher at **Poplar Elementary** before becoming the assistant principal there. Eventually, she stepped into the principal position. Poplar is a small neighborhood elementary school serving a predominantly Hispanic population. Having spent her entire career there, Janice described the school as "a well-oiled machine." Even as an undergraduate majoring in education, Janice knew she wanted to work in the service of "helping people." After several years of teaching, she discovered an interest in administration, and this pursuit was nurtured by her former principal, who supported her throughout her subsequent training and during the application process. Janice explained that the principalship suits her individual strengths and identity as someone who is "a people person" and adept at "dealing with people and building relationships." She acknowledged that "you can't do it by yourself" and made it a priority to support her staff—not just teachers, but everyone in the building who supports students in many different ways.

**Jennifer**, who took her first principalship at **Bur Oak Elementary**, is African American and in her early 40s. Conscious of how her own background differed from those of her students at the predominantly Hispanic elementary school, she embraced her new role with a deep sense of responsibility. Although Jennifer grew up in a family of educators, she described her education career as accidental, something she fell into after working in a corporate environment. Jennifer stepped into the principal role after several years of teaching experience and work as an instructional coach in a different school in the city. She was attracted to Bur Oak, a school that had been on probation for several years in a row, because of what she saw as a disparity between high teacher quality and low test scores. Motivated to make a difference, Jennifer felt that it was "a great place to come and make improvements." She described herself as a nontraditional principal and explained she has "an ethical imperative to do what is necessary to help the children of this community."

**Kathy**, Caucasian and in her 40s, grew up in a family of educators and never seriously considered any other profession. With both public and private school teaching experience, Kathy eventually moved into a school leadership position, and with encouragement from colleagues, family, and friends, she decided to pursue the certification necessary to become a principal. She got her first principal position at **Nyssa Elementary**, a school she had worked in as both a teacher and assistant principal. She explained that the development of others, both teachers and students, was central to how she thinks about the principalship.

**Nathan**, 30-something and Caucasian, began his principal career at **Spruce Elementary** after three years of teaching and various administrative positions. He worked as an assistant principal for a brief time before taking on the principalship at Spruce and was pursuing a doctoral degree in school administration during the study. Having been inspired by childhood experiences with numerous family members who were educators, Nathan sought a career that would let him "help kids make decisions—and do something good with their life, whether it's college or work or just decision-making ability." In seeking out principal positions, Nathan actively looked for schools that were in turnaround so that he could help rebuild them. Instead, he ended up at Spruce, a new school where he had an opportunity to hire his own staff and set a new vision.

(Continued)

**Figure 1.** Meet the Principals (*continued*)

**Nelson**, African American and in his 30s, became the principal at **Birch Elementary** after four years of assistant principal experience and several years of teaching. Born and raised in Chicago, Nelson graduated from a local high school and started his career in the school district as a coach and physical education teacher. He recalled being bored as a student in grade school, but things changed when he got to high school, where a new school principal with a background as a physical education teacher helped Nelson see how administration might be a way to pursue his passion. Nelson viewed the principalship as an opportunity to combine his interests in leadership and athletics. He explained his mission as influencing children so they can be successful members of society, and was troubled that he had to "fight" to get his students "fundamental exposures to simple things like preschool."

**Octavio**, Hispanic and in his 40s, moved to Chicago from Latin America in his youth and became principal at **Dogwood Elementary** after more than a decade of teaching experience in the district and a few years as Dogwood's assistant principal. A self-described lifelong learner, Octavio explained that he was drawn into education because he enjoys "sharing knowledge, information, and skills . . . and helping by coaching and modeling." He viewed academic and socioemotional learning as fundamentally integrated processes and expressed a belief in educating "the whole child." He took on the role of mentor for his students, many of whom shared similar immigration experiences. He also aimed to mentor staff and develop leadership skills in his colleagues.

**Oscar**, Hispanic and in his 40s, became principal at **Tulip Elementary** after spending almost two decades as a teacher and administrator in various schools both within and outside the United States. In his prior positions, Oscar generally attended to the instructional side of the work, and he began the principalship anticipating that the managerial aspects of the work would be a challenge. From a family of educators, Oscar trained as a teacher in his native Latin American country, and as a principal after he relocated to Chicago. Aware of his own bilingual and bicultural identity, he was determined to step up and provide leadership models for Hispanic students—and Tulip's demographics were a draw to him.

**Rich**, Caucasian and in his early 30s, became the principal at **Sevenson Elementary**, the elementary school where he had worked previously as the assistant principal. He was inspired to pursue a career in administration by negative experiences as a teacher in a school where he didn't see eye to eye with his principal. At Sevenson, Rich was excited by the opportunity to shake things up and pursue a new direction for the school. He viewed the principal role as "being a coach, being a mentor, a strong-handed leader when need be. It's about being able to match a vision with a reality that you bring about."

**Samantha**, African American and in her mid-30s, became the principal of **Sweetgum Elementary**, a newly established school, after nearly a decade of teaching experience and several years of administrative experience. Influenced by her mother's philosophy that "everybody should be a teacher at least for some amount of time," Samantha followed in the footsteps of many of her family members who are also educators. After completing her principal training and in the midst of pursuing her doctorate, she was enjoying her work as an assistant principal but decided that she "couldn't pass up" the opportunity to start a new school guided by her own vision. Owing to the support she received from mentors and her own skills in collaboration and management, Samantha felt prepared for the role in terms of both her vision and her organizational skills. As the principal of a new school, she was responsible for hiring many staff in a short time and focused on maintaining her vision during a period of rapid growth.

We draw on the stories shared through semi-structured interviews conducted as part of a study in which we followed two cohorts of Chicago principals from the summer before they started as principals to either their fifth or sixth year on the job.[10] We systematically followed the experiences of these principals, mostly through interviews but also through surveys, observations, and administrative records, as they entered, managed, and adapted to their new positions. For the larger project, we interviewed 35 principals across these two cohorts of new principals.[11]

---

[10] This work was only possible through the generous support of the Spencer Foundation.
[11] See the Appendix for a brief description of our methodological approach.

Although the 11 profiled principals' crossings took different forms depending on whether they actively sought or were coaxed into the position, or were seen as insiders or outsiders, the challenges they encountered, and the ensuing dilemmas these challenges presented, were similar and, we believe, instructive. Throughout the book, we identify some of the core challenges that principals encounter related to responsibility, stakeholder demands, time management, staff cooperation and coordination, shared leadership, and school safety; identify associated dilemmas; and explore practical and pragmatic ways to manage these dilemmas through ongoing negotiations. Although we discuss ordinary problems in addition to the ongoing dilemmas, we intend our account as something of an antidote to the problem-solving mentality that tends to drive much of the work of educators and, indeed, the general culture in which we live. We are often motivated to jump headlong into implementing solutions for problems without acknowledging the unresolvable trade-offs and conflicting values at play.

We hope the stories and strategies we share in this book will support reflection and dialogue among practitioners. To that end, we have included discussion questions at the end of each chapter. *Reflection* questions prompt you to think more deeply about the experiences shared in the chapter. *Application* questions prompt you to consider how these themes apply to your own context. Finally, *Implications* questions invite you to explore how what you have read might inform your future work.

# 2

# BEARING RESPONSIBILITY

Although the opportunity to take on new challenges is a common goal for those who become principals, newcomers are often struck by how familiar many of the responsibilities seem. This is to be expected, as most new principals cross into the job from other school administrative positions. However, the "been there, done that" feeling isn't a lasting one. The first few months in the principal's office bring a deluge of new responsibilities—including the realization of bearing ultimate responsibility for the successes and failures in the school. Principals' sense of ultimate responsibility, coupled with the volume of responsibilities, surfaces a critical dilemma that they must manage in order to lead.

In this chapter, we explore how principals cope with this multifaceted *responsibility dilemma* by examining the strategies they can use to manage it and looking at the related dilemmas that these strategies surface.

## FAMILIAR RESPONSIBILITIES

Even before they take an administrative position, most new principals have long, mostly informal apprenticeships to the principal's job. Served when they were classroom teachers or students themselves, this "apprenticeship of observation" offers a perspective on the position's day-to-day, public-facing responsibilities.[1]

---

[1] In *Schoolteacher* (1975), Dan Lortie describes the "apprenticeship of observation" to teaching that educators have through their experiences as students in the education system.

New principals' informal apprenticeships are supplemented by the somewhat more formal ones served in school leadership positions, such as assistant principal. As Kathy explained, her assistant principal position at Nyssa Elementary allowed her to practice many aspects of the principal job with the help of her mentor. When she began her own principal position, she was initially confident she'd seen it all; one year later, she reported realizing that certain aspects of the job could only be fully experienced from the principal's office.

Nyssa is located on Chicago's North Side, and it enrolls nearly equal numbers of African American, Caucasian, and Hispanic students as well as a handful of Asian students. Although the school is situated in a relatively affluent neighborhood, just over half of the student body is eligible for free or reduced-price lunch. Kathy's assistant principal experience at Nyssa eased her transition to the principal position in several ways. She recalled that as an assistant principal, she had shared responsibility with the principal for much of the "grunt work," including overseeing discipline and transportation. Her principal had also encouraged her to take an instructional leadership role. Kathy said that as an AP, she had learned that "the only way you can know the strengths and weaknesses of your staff is to be in those classrooms almost on a daily basis." She and her predecessor had worked as a team, and during the last several years of her tenure as an assistant principal, she was able to take the lead in many parts of running the school.

Even with years of experience at Nyssa, Kathy's apprenticeship didn't prepare her for all aspects of the principal's job. Three months in, she explained that a consequence of having focused so much on instructional leadership as an assistant principal was that there were several areas of the principalship she did not yet understand—among them, budgeting and personnel issues. As she put it, "I was kind of sheltered from all that. I had to learn a lot in the last five, six weeks. A ton. And it's not as scary as I thought!"

George, a young Caucasian principal new to Buckthorn Elementary, felt his formal apprenticeship as part of a principal residency "prepared him well" for the work ahead. When he took the helm at Buckthorn, the school, located on Chicago's South Side, was on probation due to low student performance.

Its study body was nearly 100 percent African American, and almost all of the students were eligible for free or reduced-price lunch. When interviewed during his first few weeks at Buckthorn, George noted the similarities in demographics and challenges between Buckthorn and the site where he completed his residency—an advantage. But he also recognized that his limited experience (just a few years of teaching and his principal training) meant that he was being exposed to certain aspects of the job for the first time and that he would need to do quite a bit of learning on the job. As George explained, "The last two days, half my day has been doing budgeting, fund transfers, and staffing things. You know—all that operations and management stuff that you just have to learn as you go."

Samantha is an African American woman who began her principal career developing a new school, Sweetgum, dedicated to providing enrichment programs for a primarily African American student body. When interviewed just before Sweetgum's opening, Samantha was confident that her stint as an assistant principal had prepared her for many of the responsibilities she would have as the head of this new school. From her perspective, there was not much difference between the work she had done and the work she was about to do. As Samantha put it, her mentor was a master principal who had taught her "how to anticipate and pre-plan. There's not going to be an issue, because she taught me to always think ahead." Like George and Kathy, though, Samantha came to realize that no amount of training could have prepared her for all aspects of a principal's work.

Of course, not all experience apprenticeships that afforded the rich learning experiences Kathy, George, and Samantha enjoyed. Assistant principals' responsibilities often revolve around what several study participants referred to as "the grunt work," and this can limit their exposure to the full range of responsibilities that principals have. Octavio, a 40-something immigrant to the United States, served as an assistant principal for two years at another Chicago elementary school before he assumed the principal position at Dogwood Elementary. He explained that as an AP, he had focused primarily on student discipline and issues related to parents. Yes, he had worked directly with teachers to help them find solutions to student behavioral issues and figure out ways to work with particular parents. He had also learned a lot about how to work with students as a disciplinarian. But he noted that the principal's range of responsibilities extends far beyond these competencies.

Despite the limited scope of some apprenticeships, the new principals in our study reported having done most, some, or all of the work of principals in their prior administrative positions. They found themselves referring back to those experiences as they took on new responsibilities, drawing on the lessons they'd learned through their apprenticeships to help navigate the transition.

## MORE AND DIFFERENT RESPONSIBILITIES

Even with extensive apprenticeships for the job, the totality of the position is still a considerable adjustment for new principals. As both Kathy and Octavio pointed out, becoming a principal involves assuming not just more responsibilities but also more complex responsibilities.

Three months into the job, Octavio explained that "the responsibility doubles or triples" and offered an analogy: becoming a principal is like being newly married. He explained:

> If you are a conscientious partner, you really want to fulfill your partner's . . . not just needs, but also their wishes; you want to develop the consideration, the sensitivity, because you are part of somebody else's life as well. You spend so many hours devoted to the other that the satisfactions are big when you are able to reach and complete the goals that you have set up.

From Octavio's perspective, part of the challenge was the newness of the position, and another was the never-ending responsibilities of the job. His analogy underscores how principals' responsibilities are magnified by others' expectations and extend beyond the personal expectations they might set based on their own goals and desires.

While comparing being a new principal to beginning a marriage may be apt, it is somewhat misleading, because the expectations for new principals come not from a single partner but from multiple partners. At the end of her first year, Kathy provided a different family-based metaphor:

It's like being a parent of 500-plus people, and I don't just mean the kids. I feel like every decision I make has the potential to leave a lasting impression. So I want to make the best possible decisions to move the school forward. And that responsibility in many ways reminds me of the responsibility I feel as a parent.

Notably, Kathy and other principals reported feeling responsible for caring not just for the children in their schools but also for the various adults in the same orbit—teachers, school staff, parents, and other stakeholders. We will take up multiple stakeholders and their competing and sometimes conflicting demands in Chapter 3.

## ULTIMATE RESPONSIBILITY

Stepping into the principal's office, newcomers not only experience more and different responsibilities but also encounter the shock of bearing what we have come to call *ultimate responsibility*. Bearing ultimate responsibility means that no matter who on staff is responsible for overseeing or completing a specific task, at the end of the day, the principal is the one who owns that task and all others. For example, although an assistant principal may be in charge of student discipline, when that disciplinary plan is ineffective, the principal is the person whom parents and other stakeholders will hold responsible. Similarly, a school's 1st grade teachers may be responsible for the daily work of ensuring that 1st graders learn to read, write, and do arithmetic, but should they fail to do so, parents and district administrators will, in due course, hold the school principal accountable. The buck stops in the principal's office, meaning everything and everyone are ultimately the principal's responsibility.

Kathy, who apprenticed under a principal who made her feel like a partner, nonetheless knew that her principal was the decision maker. She anticipated that assuming ultimate responsibility for Nyssa Elementary would be "a learning experience for all of us." In an interview conducted two years into her principalship, she shared an important lesson she'd learned—the sense of ultimate responsibility does not go away:

The ultimate responsibility will always lie at the principal's feet. Even with the assistant principal and principal working together, and as collaborative as that is, at the end of the day, the responsibility is still only the principal's. I didn't understand this until I became a principal.

Kathy went on to say that building relationships with other principals who have experienced this same ultimate responsibility is important and valuable, because they understood.

Similarly, Samantha came to see the biggest difference between being an assistant principal and being the principal as knowing that everything is her responsibility at the end of the day. At Sweetgum, she instituted a team approach to decision making by actively involving several other members of her staff behind the scenes in the work of addressing particular challenges. Samantha was happy to share the praise for these successes, but she pointed out that any failures would eventually fall on her. "If you bomb, it's you," she said. "If it goes wrong, it's on you."

The situation was similar for Janice, the principal of Poplar Elementary, a magnet school in a predominantly Hispanic neighborhood. As an AP, Janice had been charged with overseeing most of the technical work of running a school, including budgeting and hiring staff. But, as she noted with a laugh, "There was always somebody else who was ultimately responsible for it— the principal. I might have done it, but I wasn't responsible for the outcome."

All that changed when Janice became the principal. If the budget failed to add up or a new position played out in undesirable ways for staff and students, she was responsible. In an interview conducted while she was rolling out several new initiatives related to the instructional program, including the Common Core and teacher evaluation processes, Janice revealed that she felt that responsibility keenly. Although both district policymakers and her leadership team supported these initiatives, Janice still believed it fell to her to ensure the initiatives' success at Poplar.

Principals' sense of ultimate responsibility is about more than simply taking the blame should something go wrong. It has to do with their sense of commitment to the schools they lead and to the people these schools serve and employ. It is tied to their sense of social obligation for the well-being of not only the students enrolled in their schools but also staff, parents, and even the broader communities their schools serve.

Janice entered the principalship believing her primary responsibility to be students' academic success, so this demand to be a jack-of-all-trades was an unexpected challenge. In an interview conducted at the end of her first year, she reported being surprised by how different stakeholders wanted to involve the school in general, and the principal in particular, in addressing different community issues that went beyond student learning and development. As an example, she cited efforts by community groups and parents to enlist her help in responding to concerns about lead levels in the neighborhood's air.

Recognizing that she could not afford to alienate community stakeholders but also believing she needed to keep her focus on teaching, learning, and student success, Janice had the school tested for lead levels, and several tests turned up no reason for concern. In this way, she was able to assure parents and community groups that at least the air in the school was free from lead contamination. Still, some community groups continued to lobby her to take action on the broader issue. Janice noted that when she pressed parents as to what they thought she could do, they offered little guidance. The experience helped Janice realize that community concerns must be her concerns too, at least to a certain degree. At the same time, she realized she could not take on every community issue. Janice explained it as having to "walk a fine line."

George also remarked on how responsibility felt "magnified and com-pounded" in his new position as the principal of Buckthorn. Shifting from second or third in command to being fully responsible for everything and everyone—children and staff—was something of a shock. In an interview conducted a few weeks before Buckthorn would begin its first school year under his leadership, George said,

> One thing that really was smacking me in the gut Sunday night was the responsibility part. It's the ultimate responsibility. All the people who work in this building—their employment and welfare or their well-being financially is dependent upon my successful leadership of this organization. There's a lot of responsibility there.

It's a point worth underlining: dealing with problems related to families, students, and staff requires principals to make judgment calls and resolve tough issues that they have to take full responsibility for, live with, and ultimately own regardless of how things turn out.

For principals like George, who see the position as an opportunity to take on challenging work and grow professionally, ultimate responsibility brings great rewards but also no shortage of challenges. As George explained, "I find the autonomy of that empowering and rewarding. I don't have to answer to somebody for every decision I make. As long as things are going well and I'm not screwing up, I'm captain of the ship." Being ultimately responsible invigorated George as an educator but also meant additional stress. Ultimate responsibility brings the more challenging and fulfilling work that newcomers hope to find in the principal's office, and at the same time it can feel overwhelming. As George summed up, "It is both rewarding and stressful."

Managing the multiplication of professional responsibilities while also dealing with a deep sense of being ultimately responsible for the success or failure of everything that goes on within the school is one of a principal's most pressing and enduring challenges, and it surfaces what we call the *responsibility dilemma*. The sheer volume of a principal's responsibilities is such that one person cannot possibly tackle them all single-handedly, but the sense of being ultimately responsible makes it difficult to share the load with others.[2] Principals recognize they can't do it all, but they feel they need to have a hand in everything because it is they who are ultimately responsible.

## STRATEGIES FOR MANAGING RESPONSIBILITY

Principals can manage the multiplying responsibilities of the position and navigate the responsibility dilemma by employing three key strategies: accepting the managerial aspects of the job along with the instructional ones, delegating responsibility to others on staff, and sharing decision making. At the

---

[2] Note that this is a *dilemma* rather than a *problem;* it's a challenge that principals cannot solve but rather must cope with, or manage, long term.

same time, these coping strategies surface other dilemmas, which also require ongoing negotiation. It's important that principals learn to manage the dilemmas associated with shifting responsibilities, because these dilemmas do not fade away with time or experience. They remain a defining aspect of being the principal.

## Tackle the Managerial Along with the Instructional

George explained at the end of his second year as principal that one way of coping with ultimate responsibility is to accept management as a big part of the job. Over his first two years as the principal, he became increasingly aware of the importance of the day-to-day operational aspects of the work, despite all the talk about instructional leadership being the most important thing. He put it this way:

> Fiscal management and human management and facilities management—all those hats are critical too. Keeping the doors open and keeping people safe and making sure people get paid—the principal has ultimate responsibility for all those things.

George always believed instructional leadership was important, but being a principal helped him appreciate the managerial aspects of the work, often portrayed as a secondary concern. George said that dealing with ultimate responsibility involved not only accepting but also acquiescing to and attending to the managerial aspects of the principal's job, as well as seeking ways to fulfill the duty of instructional oversight.

Most newcomers enter the principal position with a deep commitment to the instructional aspects of the work, and they carry out this commitment by prioritizing instructional leadership. However, principals' desire to focus on instruction and leading its improvement is in perpetual tension with what Larry Cuban (1988) calls the "managerial imperative."[3] For Kathy, this took getting used to. Early in her first year, she complained, "The financial

---

[3] Cuban's 1988 book *The Managerial Imperative and the Practice of Leadership in Schools* examines how managerial constraints shape the work of both principals and teachers.

responsibilities—the imposition of all of that—has taken me away from what I thought I would be spending a lot of time doing: working on instruction." Over time, however, she came to accept this aspect of the work. In her second year, she explained that being a good principal means providing "the leadership needed for the teachers, keeping up with educational best practices, and knowing how to address those academic needs, while at the same time balancing the management end." For Kathy, managing the responsibility dilemma involved coping with another dilemma—balancing the managerial and the instructional.

The sense of ultimate responsibility principals feel means that most learn to acknowledge, accept, and even embrace the managerial components of the job. They don't abandon their instructional leadership ambitions; they could hardly afford to do so in an environment where policymakers use student achievement metrics to gauge school and principal performance. Moreover, principals' sense of social obligation would make it difficult, if not impossible, to abandon the instructional concerns, as they value instruction as a key way to improve the lives of students. Instead, they seek ways to balance the managerial and instructional leadership aspects of the job. "The instructional leadership part is a little bit more important than the management part, but I get that they have to go hand in hand," Kathy said. "In order to be an effective leader, you have to have a hold of that management. Finding that balance is critical."

Indeed, striving to balance instructional leadership and managerial oversight over the long haul is an essential way of coping with the responsibility dilemma. It's also a continuous struggle, and many principals never achieve perfect equilibrium. All too often, plans to spend a morning observing classroom teaching or modeling a new strategy are interrupted mid-activity (or even before the activity gets under way) by a pressing and unanticipated managerial issue—anything from a schoolyard incident to a concerned parent who refuses to speak with anyone but the principal. Principals' sense of ultimate responsibility means that ignoring the managerial is not an option. Scholars tend to privilege the instructional, and increasingly, policymakers do so as well, but principals in the field come to accept the managerial as inevitable and important. Providing sufficient attention to both is a dilemma of its own, and the work necessary to navigate it is ongoing.

## Delegate Responsibility to Others on Staff

Samantha, who began her principal career by creating a new school, acknowledged it was "absolutely impossible to do everything yourself; you have to get better at delegating." She also recognized the challenge of delegating important work to others when one is ultimately responsible. Samantha explained that her school, Sweetgum, takes a "team approach" to the work of leading and managing instruction, which means she can gather new insights and input from staff in her building. This eases the load she bears and also engages staff in initiatives they might not otherwise support.

Still, while delegating responsibility helps principals cope with the responsibility dilemma, it never fully resolves it. As noted, principals are ultimately responsible for the work that they delegate to others. If the work is not performed properly, it will fall to them to pick up the pieces. As Samantha pointed out, "You can delegate as much as you want, but you have to watch things closely, because in the end it's going to come back to you." This means part of delegating tasks is setting a performance standard, monitoring the work to ensure it meets the standard, and taking follow-up action if it is not.

When George, several years into his principalship at Buckthorn, tried to delegate responsibility to a group of teachers, he soon saw it wasn't going well and mulled over the kinds of intervention he might have to take. "I've got to rethink it," he said. "Do I need to step in more, micromanage it more?" As this comment illustrates, delegating responsibility does not mean the principal gets to walk away and focus on other things. Indeed, many principals are reluctant to "let go" because they're worried about how well "someone else" will do the work.

New principals who come from outside the school face the additional challenge of figuring out staff capabilities. Who has the skill and expertise necessary to take on which tasks? Whom can they trust to do the work well and according to schedule? As we will examine in more detail in Chapter 6, sharing the leadership load can help temper the sheer volume of work, but it does not alleviate principal's sense of being ultimately responsible.

## Share Decision Making

A related strategy for managing responsibility involves engaging others in decision making. Whereas delegation allows principals to unload particular tasks, sharing decision making engages others in leadership more directly. By establishing and supporting leadership teams composed of teachers and other staff, principals can rely on others to make recommendations about curriculum, changes to school policies, and other decisions. Neither strategy completely resolves the responsibility dilemma, but shared decision making is notable for its effectiveness in helping to mitigate the burden of ultimate responsibility.

Engaging in collaborative decision making surfaces another dilemma for school principals, especially those who have relatively clear visions for improving and transforming their schools. They have to balance giving others a voice and respecting their role in the decision-making process while also ensuring that their vision for the school is not undermined by others' decisions.

Reflecting on efforts to create a culture of collective decision making during her first five years as the principal of Nyssa, Kathy noted, "There were times it bit me in the butt!" She recalled going along with decisions made by her leadership team despite her personal reservations and realizing later that doing so had been the wrong call.

On the one hand, principals who create opportunities for shared decision making value collaboration and engaging others in leadership. On the other hand, they are typically committed to a particular vision for transforming their school, which may differ from the visions of other stakeholders. Principals who override the outcomes of shared decision making to advance their own ambitions for school improvement run the risk of undermining the entire shared decision-making effort, alienating those involved, and defeating the entire purpose of sharing decision making.

One tool for managing the dilemma that emerges from shared decision making is setting and modeling norms. Over time, Kathy learned to identify non-negotiables—parts of the school mission and plans she was not prepared to compromise on. This clarity enabled her to figure out when to stand her ground and when to cede decisions to the collective. She explained that listening in order to understand where others—especially others with contrary views and positions—were truly coming from was critical.

For Samantha, getting better at engaging others in the work was key to managing the responsibility dilemma. She modeled for her staff how to handle certain situations, hoping that this would lead them to execute their responsibilities "in the way that's in the best interest of the students and of the school." She clarified that this wasn't a foolproof approach, though,

> because nothing is cut and dry in a school. There's no textbook answer. Nothing to say, "In Situation A, you always do this, and in Situation B, you do this." It's where the gray area is that you feel like you're really trusting a great deal that people on your team are going to act in a way that's best for kids and parents and teachers.

Still, Samantha believed that with enough modeling, the Sweetgum staff would come to know "how we as a school have to approach parent conflicts and student conflicts . . . in the way that's in line with our vision." Until that point, she said, she would continue checking in with those entrusted with decision making so she could "keep a finger on the pulse" and know what is going on.

Another tool for principals is mindset adjustment. Samantha acknowledged that when all is said and done, a principal also has to let go and accept that "mistakes are going to happen and it's not the end of the world. If it goes wrong, it's fixable."

The multiplicity of responsibilities in the principal's office, together with an enduring sense of being ultimately responsible for all the school's operations and outcomes, poses a dilemma that principals must manage in order to lead. For newcomers, the task can feel overwhelming. Fortunately, there are a number of effective strategies to deploy, including balancing the managerial aspects of the job while attending to the instructional ones, delegating responsibility, and sharing decision making.

Although these strategies are crucial in managing the overarching responsibility dilemma, they surface other dilemmas, including tensions between the instructional and the managerial aspects of the job, releasing control in delegating responsibility while trying to ensure things are done in an acceptable way, and balancing one's own ideas about improvement with the ideas of those with whom they share responsibility.

## Discussion Questions

1. *Reflection:* Kathy described feeling torn between managerial and instructional responsibilities, but also acknowledged that these responsibilities are not always distinct. Can you think of an example of when the two might go hand in hand?

2. *Application:* One of the challenges with sharing decision making is that principals are ultimately responsible for the outcome, regardless of their role in the decision. Can you think of a time when you had to take responsibility for a decision you did not make? How did you navigate this? How was the situation resolved?

3. *Implications:* For new principals, adjusting to the sense of ultimate responsibility that comes with entering the principal's office is often a struggle. How might new principals be supported over their first few years on the job to help them adjust to this unique challenge? How might school districts anticipate and scaffold this adjustment?

# 3

# DIVERSE STAKEHOLDERS

Not only are principals ultimately responsible; they are ultimately responsible to many stakeholders.

According to Nelson, the Chicago-born, African American appointed to lead Birch Elementary, a good principal is someone who meets the needs of *all* stakeholders—from students to staff to families to community members. This is a lofty ambition, but Nelson is not alone in his embrace of it. At the end of her first year as principal of Bur Oak Elementary, Jennifer pointed out that a good principal has to be able to balance attention among all stakeholders. While she saw her primary responsibility as supporting the student body, this was something she could not do on her own. Jennifer explained that the accumulation of input from teachers, paraprofessionals, district policymakers, community members, politicians, and even the students themselves necessarily drives that work that principals do. Comparing her position to that of a CEO of a company who has to balance the day-to-day work with longer-term goals, Jennifer was clear that her success depended on attending to the needs of both internal and external stakeholders.

Managing diverse stakeholders' expectations and negotiating the push and pull of their various demands raises dilemmas for principals, including honoring one stakeholder group while not alienating another, being responsive to stakeholders while maintaining a coherent principal persona and agenda, and balancing the need for transparency with the requirement for confidentiality.

In this chapter, we will explore these dilemmas and present some strategies for navigating them.

## INTERNAL STAKEHOLDERS

Principals focus much of their attention on internal stakeholders: students, teachers, and other staff members. Even before Jennifer signed her principal contract, she conducted an "informal survey" of the Bur Oak teaching staff in order to get a sense of what they thought the new school year's priorities should be. But attending to stakeholders is not entirely a matter of principals' choice. Stakeholders insist on getting the principal's ear. Jennifer recalled how, when she started the job, every teacher in the school wanted to talk with her so that she would get to know them and their particular take on Bur Oak's history.

Internal stakeholders also set high expectations for newcomers to the principal's office, especially for those who come from outside. Jennifer, who did not have a history at Bur Oak, recalled,

> I will never forget when the office clerk said, "You know, we've all been really waiting for someone like you. We hope that you will give us a change that we so desperately need." And I'm thinking, *I'm not Obama! They think I'm going to be some kind of savior!*

She quickly realized that the school's internal stakeholders held lofty and somewhat improbable expectations of her ability to immediately improve the instructional program and get Bur Oak off probation. Jennifer understood that securing staff support was the only way she could hope to realize these goals. As she explained, "When you're making cultural changes or structural changes, you need buy-in from the staff; you need to make sure that you're looking at all stakeholders and how they would be impacted by the changes that you're making." Gaining staff cooperation and coordinating stakeholder efforts are central concerns for principals; we will discuss this in detail in Chapter 5.

For Kathy, the former assistant principal at Nyssa who became its new principal, responding to teachers' expectations presented a different kind of challenge. In her former role, she was always available for teachers when they wanted to talk, and this contributed to the widespread staff support she received when she applied for the principal position. In an interview prior to her start date, Kathy expressed trepidation about how her new role would affect internal stakeholder expectations of her:

> It's going be a whole new culture. They're going to be used to coming in this door. I'm concerned about that challenge of putting in limits so I can get things done—be out there and not wind up stuck in my office because they're all coming to me.

Kathy explained that she wanted to talk to and interact with her staff regularly, but the demands of the position required her to draw some new boundaries. The constant availability she offered as an assistant principal was no longer an option for a principal with ultimate responsibility. The dilemma she faced was continuing to be accessible to staff (which she saw as essential to helping her achieve her ambitions for Nyssa) while somehow restricting staff access to protect her time so she could attempt to stay on top of the crush of new responsibilities (which would possibly alienate these crucial stakeholders).

## EXTERNAL STAKEHOLDERS

In addition to managing adults within the school building, principals must maintain functional relationships with parents and members of the wider community. Of all a school's external stakeholders, parents often get the lion's share of a principal's time and attention. Jennifer noted that during her first month on the job, she had 25 conversations with different external stakeholders, mainly parents. She also met with members of the locally elected school council—including parents, past and present—to discuss numerous concerns about the school. She explained that members of a particular group, composed of both parents *and* school council members, were eager to assert influence and shape the school. Jennifer pointed out that she was not so easily swayed, but she recognized the political aspect of the work and listened carefully to the group's concerns. She was in a tricky position, as she needed to listen and respond but did not want to be perceived as bending to one or another set of demands.

Parents are a crucial stakeholder in all schools, whereas the attention a principal provides to other external stakeholders often varies according to a school's particular circumstances. In schools that are on the district's watch list due to poor student performance and attendance, school district policy-makers tend to be more involved. When Nelson began his principal career at Birch, a school that had been on probation for several years, he was acutely aware of his accountability to district administrators. "The district expects my numbers—my data—to reflect a successful school. They want change to be evident in my statistics," he explained. Birch's circumstances made district administrators key stakeholders for Nelson to manage, but not the only stakeholders. He also reported feeling accountable to parents and community members in addition to students and teachers. His metric for measuring the feelings of these stakeholders wasn't the set statistics he would be providing to district administrators; it was collective pride in Birch.

The challenge new principals face mediating the demands of external stakeholders is affected by the expectations established by previous principals. In Jennifer's case, the biggest challenge was shifting the expectations of parents, who were accustomed to having a strong influence on day-to-day activities at Bur Oak Elementary. As an African American, Jennifer acknowledged feeling like something of an outsider in the primarily working-class community of Hispanic immigrants her school served.

Under Bur Oak's previous principal, a handful of parents had been very involved in school activities—disruptively so, from the perspectives of many teachers. Jennifer explained the issue as she came to understand it:

> There are a couple of parents in the building who actually ran the school. They would collect school funds for activities, come in and tell the clerk, office staff, security, and the engineer what to do. They would even observe teachers on a regular basis.

She explained that it upset Bur Oak teachers that parents of students in the primary grades would walk their children into the classroom, sit down, and not leave. Jennifer remembered a teacher coming to her during her first month on the job and explicitly saying, "I want you to do something about these parents who are harassing us all the time. Will you stand up for us?"

This is an example of how a key set of internal stakeholders (teachers) may seek a principal's assistance managing a key group of external stakeholders (parents). Bur Oak teachers asked Jennifer to establish new, clear expectations about parental involvement, including regulating parents' access to the classrooms. They expected Jennifer to take their side, even though that would create a conflict with parents.

## THE PERILS OF TAKING SIDES

Taking sides is risky for principals. They depend on multiple stakeholders and cannot be seen to be ignoring or undervaluing anyone's demands and expectations. The challenge of responding to some stakeholders without alienating others is what we call the *diplomacy dilemma*.

Jennifer valued both parental involvement and teachers having uninterrupted time for classroom instruction. She knew that to succeed as principal, she needed the support of both parents and teachers. Ultimately, Jennifer chose to invoke school board policy on parental involvement while enthusiastically encouraging parent volunteerism, telling them, "Parents, we appreciate you being here; we welcome you; we want to be your partners." She required all volunteers to fill out district-mandated paperwork, complete background checks, and follow a schedule. When some parents complained that they had always been able to visit their child's classroom whenever they wanted, Jennifer explained to them, "This is a new year. We want to do what's right by the children, to ensure the safety of all of our children in the building." Through these actions and explanations, Jennifer grounded her response in students' best interests rather than siding with one stakeholder group over another.

Navigating stakeholders' demands is not just a managerial or instructional task; it's also a political one. Recognizing this, Jennifer decided to manage expectations by reaching out to other community leaders. Notably, she met with the state representative and the local alderman to begin building a coalition of support. Jennifer explained that her aim was to help various stakeholders feel more at ease. "Even though I'm a new person here, I still want to respect some of the values and the traditions that made this school a great school," she said.

Jennifer admitted to feeling like an outsider during her early days at Bur Oak. But even principals who feel they are representative of the communities they serve, and even those who have worked in other positions at the school prior to assuming the principal position, report feeling overwhelmed by the challenge of attending to the concerns and demands of various stakeholders. As Kathy explained at the end of her first year as the principal of Nyssa,

> At times it's hard to accommodate it all. Sometimes you have to pick and choose, and one aspect is going to get more of me than another. That's just how it is. It's sort of like at home; sometimes one family member just needs more. You know, I learned from the previous principal that fair is not always equal.

Several principals in the study echoed Kathy's analogy of needing to divide attention among multiple family members based on fluctuations of need. At the same time, they recognized that some stakeholders have the wherewithal to command more attention than others—such as the parents who are more vocal than others and know how to get the attention of principals, district administrators, and local politicians.

## CONSISTENCY IN THE FACE OF STAKEHOLDER PUSH AND PULL

Managing the diplomacy dilemma—striving to respond to the demands of one stakeholder group without alienating other stakeholders who may have conflicting demands—raises another dilemma for principals. They must balance the need to respond to different stakeholders' expectations while presenting a coherent professional persona and agenda. We call this the *consistency dilemma*.

This dilemma can be particularly acute for new principals who are actively working to establish themselves and build trust. Treating different stakeholders and groups differently can give the appearance of being weak or being unfair. Tschannen-Moran's (2014) work on the principal–teacher relationship reinforces how establishing trust is crucial yet sometimes difficult in the face of conflicting stakeholder demands.[1]

At the end of her first year at Nyssa Elementary, Kathy described "being pulled in all different directions and trying to meet the needs of everybody" as one of the toughest parts of her job. Like many new principals, Kathy wanted to please everyone and soon found herself worn out from trying to do so. Efforts to juggle the various demands of different stakeholders include trying to perform a multiplicity of roles and take on a range of personas. Nelson, the principal at Birch, described it as being "a jack-of-all-trades—a mother, a father, a doctor, a nurse, a counselor, a business manager, a mediator, a lawyer, a teacher, and a master teacher." At times these different roles conflict with one another.

"Some principals can seem kind of all over the place," Nelson remarked when describing his struggle to present a consistent self to his stakeholders. He worried that they would be confused about who he really was and where he was trying to take the school. While some principals accept the chameleon-like nature of the work, others (like Nelson) strive to present a coherent and consistent self even across stakeholders. It is never easy.

## TRANSPARENCY AND DISCRETION

For Nelson and others, the consistency dilemma goes hand in hand with the *transparency dilemma:* figuring out how to balance the need for transparency with the need to maintain a certain level of confidentiality. Nelson explained that he values transparency as a means of establishing authenticity in his interactions. He described a time when he realized a veteran teacher was resisting retirement, hanging on for financial reasons. He knew this teacher's retirement would be in the best interest of the students and the school, and he was able

---

[1] Tschannen-Moran (2014) describes trusting relationships as important for getting the work of leadership done.

to work with her and convince her the time had come. He was certain that his honesty and transparency were the keys to the situation's successful resolution. He had a good relationship with this veteran teacher; she trusted him and his advice.

Transparency, though essential to building trust with stakeholders, can surface a dilemma for principals who are constrained by legal circumstances or privacy concerns from making all the details of a decision public. For example, principals in the study reported having fired teachers for reasons that they could not discuss, and then having to deal with the consequences from their staff who demanded to know why a favored colleague was let go. Managing the transparency dilemma requires principals to selectively maintain confidentiality while positioning themselves as authentic, open, and communicative.

## CONFLICTING AND COMPETING DEMANDS

Principals must also publicly deal with stakeholders who place distinct and sometimes conflicting demands on them and on their schools. For example, Kathy mentioned how some Nyssa parents set expectations for teachers that were unrealistic and undermined her responsibility to protect teachers' time. "It's not unheard of for our parents to expect teachers to stay after school and do tutoring, and a lot of them will do it," Kathy explained. "But if they can't, they can't. Some of our teachers are in graduate school; some have young families." Kathy also pointed out how Nyssa's parents, who are "hypervigilant about making sure" their children can get into the best high schools, can come into conflict with teachers over grades. She found herself needing to defend and protect her teachers while simultaneously reassuring parents that she valued them and their children.

Though the particulars were different, Jennifer also managed competing demands from teacher and parent stakeholders at Bur Oak and felt real pressure to "take sides" in a conflict between these groups. As described earlier, staff at Bur Oak had high hopes that Jennifer would "stand up" for them and bring what they saw as a necessary change: curtailing parent access to classrooms. At the same time, the Bur Oak parents wanted to maintain the status quo, which meant unrestricted access to their children's classrooms. Faced with the diplomacy dilemma, Jennifer had to determine how to respond to this pressure from teachers without losing the trust of parents.

Conflicts *within* stakeholder groups can also present dilemmas. A common example is when principals find themselves challenged to manage opposing demands from distinct groups of parents. When Octavio took over as principal of Dogwood, the surrounding neighborhood, undergoing gentrification, was roughly half white and half Hispanic. However, the student body at Dogwood was mostly Hispanic and from low-income families. Nearly 50 percent of them were English language learners. Aware that the neighborhood's gentrification was likely to continue, Octavio reasoned that to maintain enrollments at Dogwood, he would need to reach out to more of the affluent newer residents and figure out how to entice them to enroll their children in Dogwood rather than a private school. At the same time, he needed to develop a compelling program that would appeal to parents whose children already attended Dogwood. Octavio's primary challenge here was not managing conflicting demands from two different stakeholder groups but figuring out how to appeal to two very distinct groups within the same key set of stakeholders.

## STRATEGIES FOR MANAGING STAKEHOLDER CHALLENGES

Principals can manage the dilemmas that arise from grappling with stakeholders' diverse and often conflicting demands by drawing on a set of strategies that can help them balance others' expectations. As we'll see, although these strategies are ways to cope with the dilemmas, they can sometimes bring other dilemmas to the surface.

### Center Children

Centering children is a way for principals to focus their attention on what matters most when entertaining and exploring stakeholders' multiple or competing demands. It means weighing what is owed to children against all else. As Jennifer told her local school council, "I have an ethical responsibility to do what is necessary to help the children of this community. If I have to compromise that to appease someone's personal goals that have nothing to do with the kids, then I will give up the principalship and go back to being a teacher."

Kathy established a similar stance wherein doing "what's best for the students" was the bottom line—the primary responsibility for her and her staff. At the start of her first year as principal, Kathy explained that she and her staff were at Nyssa to serve, and that her central role was to ensure that Nyssa was "a safe place where kids are valued, and their educational needs are identified." Being "socially and emotionally present for the kids" was a top priority. At the end of that first year, she remained convinced of the importance of anchoring and arbitrating decisions based on the needs of children. As she put it, "The kids *really* have to be part of every decision." She offered as an example how she chose among the 20 applicants for an open special education position: it came down to who she believed to be the most committed to and connected with children.

Principals can use the "center children" strategy to not only sort through stakeholder demands and decide which demands to act on and which to push back on, but also to negotiate among competing stakeholder demands. At Nyssa, when a parent complained that her son had been made to stand in the corner and face the wall as punishment, Kathy had no difficulty adjudicating the situation. "I am here to support you," Kathy informed the teacher who doled out this punishment, "but I can't allow a kid to be treated that way. It's not going to fly." She went on to arrange for a restorative justice circle involving the teacher, the student, the parent, herself, the assistant principal, and the counselor in an effort to repair the relationship. Kathy noted how disappointing it was that the teacher seemed "very reluctant to take any ownership of the bad choices that she made." She was also upset by the teacher's inability to name something about the child that she really liked and by her general negativity throughout the circle meeting. This was especially jarring because the student had been quick to identify the teacher's sense of humor as something he liked about her and had apologized for being disrespectful. Kathy explained that the teacher involved was a good teacher—personable and valuable as a staff member; however, the bottom line for her in negotiating the conflict was doing what's best for students. This was the filter through which she examined all stakeholder demands.

While centering children helps principals manage dilemmas that arise from stakeholders' challenging and sometimes conflicting demands, it is at best an imperfect strategy. Not everyone will always agree on what is best for children. Parents' view of this can differ wildly from a teacher's perspective. Consider that what a parent thinks is best for his or her own child can come into conflict with what other stakeholders believe to be best for the other children in the classroom. Further, no stakeholder group is monolithic in its views on what is best for children; parents often disagree with one another about what children should learn and how they learn best, as do teachers and other stakeholders. Further still, what may be best for children may come at too great a cost for other stakeholders, such as teachers. Think of the parents at Nyssa who asked teachers to stay after school to tutor their children. While Kathy recognized the benefit that this might have for students, she also recognized the burden it would create for teachers enrolled in graduate coursework or with young children at home. Having exhausted, burned-out, or resentful teachers might ultimately come back around to negatively impact students. You can see how "center children" is by no means a silver bullet.

## Grease the Squeaky Wheel

New principals should focus less on external stakeholders' general power and influence at the school and more on these stakeholders' specific demands—especially demands that conflict with their own goals for the school. This practical "grease the squeaky wheel" approach is a way to cope with conflicts by keeping stakeholders somewhat satisfied, or at least letting them know they are getting attention.[2]

Nelson devoted much attention to Birch's parents during his first year as principal, and he was particularly attentive to demands from parents who disagreed with his disciplinary decisions. Just a few months into the job,

---

[2] For a more detailed account of stakeholder relations, see Spillane and Anderson (2014) and Prado Tuma and Spillane (2019).

Nelson had to respond to a parent who argued that her daughter—who had been barred from attending the school dance as punishment for fighting—should be allowed to attend the dance after all. The parent contended that another student had instigated the fight by calling her daughter a name. Nelson pointed out that the other student was also being disciplined, and he carefully explained that no matter who had started the conflict, her daughter was responsible for her own response. The punishment stood.

Nelson found that many Birch parents saw fighting as justifiable behavior that didn't merit discipline, and this attitude presented a significant challenge to his own efforts to create a peaceful learning environment. Even as he tried to establish peaceful resolutions to disagreements among students, the opposing messages from some parents required his ongoing attention. Similarly, Nelson had to work to persuade some parents to support the school's efforts to have all children wear the school uniform and follow school rules.

Greasing squeaky wheels by attending to the most vocal and conflicting demands allows principals to manage different stakeholders up to a point. However, this strategy creates other dilemmas. For one, demands from stakeholders that are consistent with the principal's goals may not rise to the level of action—they may be ignored or go unappreciated. When this happens, principals run the risk of alienating stakeholders who could provide valuable support. In addition, principals risk cultivating a culture in which more influential parents seek and expect to gain principal access and response while other parents are excluded. Further, by attending mostly to conflicting demands, principals put themselves in the position to be pulled in numerous directions and can give the impression of being reactive rather than advancing a proactive and coherent agenda. Efforts to grease the squeaky wheels, and the dilemmas that emerge from doing so, often teach principals that grease is not enough. They must also reconsider and reconstruct their sense of the principal's role and responsibilities.

## Reconsider the Principal's Role

The principalship teaches principals that it is impossible to make everyone happy all of the time and be all things to all people. As Samantha explained after several years at Sweetgum, "The only way to manage this job is know that you can't respond to everything; you must pick and choose." Referring to the demands of district administrators, she went on to say, "Some of them, you're going to defend your school against. You're going to say, 'You all can slap me on the wrist or worse, but I cannot do that. I cannot put that on my teachers.'" As she and other principals in the study gained experience, they reconstructed their own expectations for dealing with external stakeholders and worked at shifting the expectations of others. They put boundaries on what they would do in relation to external stakeholders, came to accept that part of the job entails taking unpopular positions, and set and stuck to priorities.

A number of the principals characterized this shift as dramatic. Nelson, who began his first school year at Birch convinced he needed to meet the needs of *all* stakeholders, learned to take and live with unpopular positions. For him, that meant moving forward with his agenda regardless of what his local school council thought. Midway through his first year, he reported reminding himself to let the chips fall where they may. Nelson said, "A mentor of mine told me a long time ago that as long as you focus on the kids, every-thing else will take care of itself."

For some principals, establishing boundaries involved attempts to limit commitments outside the schoolhouse. Think of Janice at Poplar resisting community organizations' efforts to involve her in neighborhood environmen-tal activism. But this strategy only goes so far, as pressures from community stakeholders are often difficult to resist. By bounding their work, principals run the risk of undermining their own and their school's legitimacy by coming across as nonresponsive. It also raises an additional dilemma, as principals seek to balance their sense of social obligation with the necessity to set bound-aries around their efforts. Despite this risk, principals' work to refine their own sense of their role and educate different stakeholders about what is and is not the school principal's responsibility is a way to manage the competing demands of different stakeholders.

In face of challenging and often conflicting stakeholder expectations, needs, and demands, principals can anchor themselves firmly, if imperfectly, by grounding their decisions in what's best for children, but they also benefit from being prepared to manage stakeholder-related dilemmas as they arise.

Principals can manage the diplomacy dilemma by trying to honor each stakeholder group without alienating any other, and they can manage the often-subsequent consistency dilemma by presenting a coherent professional persona and improvement agenda while being responsive to different stakeholders' expectations. They also must navigate the transparency dilemma as they work to build trust while honoring confidentiality requirements. Managing these dilemmas requires ongoing negotiation using coping strategies such as centering children, prioritizing responses to address the most pressing discordant voices, and redefining their sense of the principal's job.

## Discussion Questions

1. *Reflection:* Octavio was challenged to balance two distinct groups among his parent stakeholders. What advice would you give to a principal trying to appeal to the parents who have not yet opted into a school while still serving the students who are currently enrolled?

2. *Application:* Sometimes principals must decide to listen to one stakeholder at the expense of another. Can you think of a time in your professional life when you have had to navigate competing demands? What did you prioritize, and how did you decide on that course of action? If you had it to do over again, would you make the same call?

3. *Implications:* In future leadership positions, what steps might you take to help you manage the dilemmas discussed in this chapter? What decision-making processes might help you balance competing stakeholder demands? What communication approach might help you balance transparency with confidentiality?

# 4

# MANAGING TASKS AND TIME

Jennifer had expected the workload to be consuming, but three months into her first principal position, she was struck by just how consuming it was:

> Oh my god, I have never been this busy in my whole life. I don't even have time to get my hair done. I don't have time to go shopping. I haven't even bought my kids a Christmas gift because I'm here. By the time I leave at night, everything's closed, and I'm exhausted.

She had been drawn to the principalship in search of more challenging work that would help her grow professionally, and she got what she bargained for—and more.

Bur Oak Elementary had emerged from probation the year before Jennifer took over as principal, and she felt enormous pressure from the district to maintain its recently acquired "good standing" status. "Everything is about performance," she explained. "If I don't make at least 5 to 10 percentage points of an increase in student test scores, I'll be out of here. They've marched out quite a few principals."

Jennifer's sense of exhaustion is typical for those in the principal role. Managing multiple stakeholders and bearing ultimate responsibility conspire to create a chronic case of too much to do and too little time to do it. We call this the *tasking time dilemma*. In this chapter, we explore the challenge of attempting to accomplish limitless tasks in limited time and discuss strategies for managing this dilemma. We also address how these strategies surface another dilemma—that of balancing work life and home life, personal time and professional time.

## TASK OVERLOAD, TIME SHORTAGE

It would surprise few that new principals in challenging school circumstances struggle with the tasking time dilemma. But work volume and time shortages confront all who step into the principalship, whether they take the helm in high-performing or lower-performing schools.

For his first principal position, Nathan, a Caucasian man in his 30s and a former teacher, actively sought out schools where students were "behind their potential" and in need of improvement. Instead, he was hired to head Spruce, a new magnet school serving high-achieving students. Nathan later explained that he believed working at Spruce would ultimately set him up for a future principal position in a low-performing school. But even in relatively comfortable circumstances like Spruce, principals encounter constant demands on their time and a seemingly endless lists of tasks. Nathan confessed that it sometimes felt like more than he could manage. He explained that he felt he dealt with the pressure fairly well, attributing this to his laid-back personality and his tendency to "not get worked up about little stuff." But Nathan worried openly about the toll his being a principal was taking on his family life. Finding the time to stay on top of his work responsibilities meant shifting more home responsibilities to his wife. Although she was very supportive, it was draining on her to shoulder the majority of the care for their 2-year-old daughter.

At Nyssa Elementary, a high-performing, racially diverse school in a comparably affluent part of the city, Kathy also anticipated task overload and time challenges after just a month or so on the job, even before the new school year was officially under way. During her first summer, she said, "There are no kids in this building, but I could be here every night until 8 o'clock. I mean, I have to force myself to leave. I have three kids at home. Learning how to manage all this will be difficult."

Her intuition was right. Three months into the job, Kathy reported spending long hours and even weekends at Nyssa. "I was here Sunday until 11:30 at night," she noted. Of all the challenges she was facing, she identified time balance as the toughest: "I could use another four hours per day and another day of the week!"

## The Influence of Internal and External Crossing

Some newcomers, like Kathy, enter the principal position in schools where they have worked for several years as a teacher or in another administrative position. Others, like Nathan and Jennifer, come from outside, taking the helm of schools they know little about through personal experience. While both means of crossing have distinct advantages and disadvantages (see Chapter 1), we might expect insiders to have an advantage when it comes to managing work volume and time. After all, insiders have worked in the building.[1] They know the staff, students, and community already and don't need to invest time learning the ins and outs of a new environment.

Nathan came from the outside, but in a way, so did everyone at Spruce. It was a new magnet school, and Nathan had the luxury of hiring his own staff. He was grateful for this, pointing out that he was spared the new-to-the-school principal's task of figuring out "who you need to get rid of, who you can keep, who you can work with, who you can't." However, Nathan worried about adjusting to his new environment and new role. He explained he was unsure how to divide his time so that he had "a lot of time for parents, for teachers . . . time to be in classrooms every day and still work on curriculum and instruction, climate, culture." He wondered aloud how he would get everything done without burning himself out. He faced substantial work to set a learning agenda, identify the school's challenges, learn about staff's personal and interpersonal dynamics, and so on.

In contrast to Nathan, Kathy was an insider encouraged to pursue the principalship by her predecessor, with whom she had worked closely. After 10 years at Nyssa in a variety of positions, she was well liked and respected

[1] See Spillane and Lee (2014) for more detail about the process of socialization for new principals.

throughout the building. Indeed, Kathy's reputation was such that although the local school council advertised the position and received some applicants, they decided to hire Kathy without interviewing anyone else.

But even building veterans with strong relationships and knowledge of the school struggle to manage task volume and time. Kathy described spending long hours at the school fighting to stay on top of the workload. As her experience illustrates, an internal transition to the principal's office may ease the task and time challenges of becoming a principal, but it does not completely alleviate them.

## A Steep Learning Curve or a Perpetual Challenge?

Some of the task and time predicaments new principals face are undoubtedly attributable to taking on a new job. As Nathan put it, "It will very much be a learning curve." Nathan, Jennifer, and Kathy, like most new principals, served long apprenticeships to the position in other school leadership roles, which allowed them to observe the work up close. Even so, as discussed in Chapter 2, newcomers find there is still much to learn. Kathy confessed that she was unprepared for the vast array and sheer number of demands she would face. "I was the assistant principal for nine years, and I worked very closely with my predecessor. I still didn't have any idea of exactly how much of me this principal job would take," she said.

We might expect that as new principals settle into the position, the volume of work and pressure of time would lessen and perhaps disappear. However, time on the job seemed to do little to mitigate the task and time predicament these principals faced. For example, at the three-month point, Nathan reported regularly putting in 12-hour days at Spruce, entering the building at 6 a.m. and not leaving until 6 p.m. He also took work home, attending to it after his wife had turned in for the night. Two years into his principalship and with a new set of twins at home, he admitted he was still struggling to find balance between his work and family obligations.

Nathan's situation was complicated by the fact that he tried to stay on top of the job's demands by bringing work home. "It's like I can't turn off that part of my brain, " he admitted. "Even if I'm not doing something for school, some part of my brain is thinking about what I need to do." Despite this, Nathan was optimistic that one day he would find the balance he sought. Nathan's grappling with the tasking time dilemma is an ideal illustration of a common secondary dilemma: balancing the personal and professional, or what we call the *work–home dilemma*. For principals, the work is always present, even when they are away from school, at home, or with family.

Jennifer also continued to struggle with managing the volume of work. She worried about the physical toll the stress of the position was taking on her. By the end of her second year, she was wondering if she would be able to cope with the exhausting, ongoing demands. "I don't want to be in the hospital," she said. "I know a 40-year old principal who died last week, and I had another principal friend in the hospital." Yet Jennifer continued to believe she would figure out how to meet the demands of the job and carve out time to attend to her own well-being. Referring back to her colleague who passed away, she exclaimed, "I'm not going out like that!"

After two years as principal at Nyssa, Kathy was also still grappling with the workload and spent many Sundays at the school for six or eight hours. She explained that she tried to leave the building by 5 p.m. on most week-days, but there were always evenings when she was at Nyssa until 9 p.m. It was not unusual for her to put in another hour or two of work at home once her family was asleep. Still, Kathy maintained hope that with some more time and experience in the position, she would find ways to make the demands more manageable and need to spend less time working. However, three years later, at the end of her fifth year as principal, little had changed for Kathy, who was still spending long days and part of her weekends at Nyssa. "It's a 12- to 14-hour day at least Monday through Thursday," she said. "I try to get out of here by 4 o'clock on Friday, but I'm not always successful, and I usually work at least part of Saturday or Sunday." She explained that although aspects of the position had become easier over the years, navigating the tasking time dilemma was not one of them. Despite her best efforts to leave the office at the office, new challenges continually arose that required her attention.

This is an important point. Although the learning curve associated with taking on the position may be implicated in some of the time challenges new

principals encounter, the passing of time does not alleviate their time predicaments. Even after five years on the job, principals like Kathy talk about the
time they need to put in to keep a never-ending list of tasks under control. It
is not that principals don't learn from their experiences; they report learning
tremendously. But as principals gain more experience, they often take on more
and different responsibilities. In this way, increasing their own capabilities
actually leads to more work rather than less. In other words, work overload
and time shortage are more than just products of the steep learning curve that
comes with becoming a principal; they are intrinsic to the position and how
it is structured.

## CHALLENGES OF TASK AND TIME MANAGEMENT

Principals' sense of social obligation and ultimate responsibility, together with
the diverse demands of multiple stakeholders, work together to ensure that
demand for principals' time outstrips their supply. As Michael Lipsky (2010)
writes, frontline public service workers, including educators, social workers,
and police, must cope with the reality that demand for their services will be
far greater than their time and resources to provide these services.

### Obligation, Responsibility, and Stakeholders

Principals' sense of social obligation to others, especially to those who
are marginalized by society, makes it difficult to turn a blind eye to anyone
needing or seeking help from their local schoolhouse. Often it is students
whom they seek to serve, but it's also parents and even community members.
In many schools, rising poverty levels among school-age children coupled
with a shrinking social service safety net expand the gulf between stakeholder
demands and principal time to address these demands.

Some principals, especially those working in the highest-poverty areas,
find themselves stretched thin trying to support students and families. Their
sense of ultimate responsibility for the school and all whom the school serves
compounds the dilemma. Kathy linked the time crunch in part to her own
sense of ultimate responsibility. She explained that she was very careful and

methodical in her delegation because any work that does not get done or is done poorly will have lasting, perhaps devastating, effects on children and their families. Poor work—even done by someone else on staff—also reflects negatively on the principal. When they did delegate, principals said that they still tended to look over the shoulders of those they delegated to in an effort to ensure the work would get done in a way that was acceptable to them.

It is understandable that principals' sense of being ultimately responsible would contribute to their seemingly endless to-do lists and make it difficult for them to manage their time. Kathy explained that coming in on the weekends and staying late at night was related to her need for uninterrupted time to work. Her efforts to set aside sacred space for work during the school day were often thwarted by the number of people who wanted her attention. She noted, "Sometimes I have to close my door, even to parents, teachers, students, my AP, everybody." Kathy admitted that her efforts to do this often failed because she could not, in good conscience, ignore these help seekers; too much was at stake. It introduced another difficult balancing act: ignoring some stakeholders some of the time was necessary for her to find the time to serve more stakeholders well.

The complexity of the principalship helps to explain why "better time management" is not a solution to the tasking time dilemma. Principals lead public organizations that not only reside in but also depend on their external environments for their continued existence. These environments, as we saw in Chapter 3, are made up of multiple stakeholders who have expectations for their schools and place demands on school principals. A principal who ignores these stakeholders risks damaging the legitimacy of the school in the eyes of the broader community. There is no getting around the fact that attending to everyone's needs—those of parents and teachers as well as students—requires a tremendous time investment.

Several principals in the study likened their role to that of a politician. Whether they ultimately respond to stakeholders' demands or not, they have to listen, which takes time. This political aspect of the work interfaces with principals' sense of social obligation, which principals serving traditionally marginalized communities feel intensely. Their sense of responsibility and sense of purpose manifest as a perpetual demand on their time and energy. So even if Kathy could somehow get that dreamed-of "extra four hours per day" or even "another day" in the week, demands on her time would likely rise to consume those additional hours.

## Task Diversity and Unpredictability

Task diversity and the unpredictability of the work complicate the task overload and time shortage crunch. Midway through her first year as principal of Poplar Elementary, Janice offered this perspective:

> Being a jack-of-all-trades, you are the instructional leader, and that's the main thing. But you are also a social worker when someone needs a shoulder to cry on. I am also an engineer. And if parents come in with issues that they have going on at home and they want to know if they should call the police, now I'm a lawyer! You're expected to be everything to everybody.

Also consider that, for principals expected to perform these multiple roles, it is not just about taking care of the tasks they face—doing the work; it is also about developing the skills and knowledge necessary to do the work. That, too, takes time.

In an interview conducted soon after Kathy was named principal of Nyssa, before the new school year had even started, she commented that unpredictability was already part of the job. "I hit the door and never know what's going to be in front of me. I can have my day planned out perfectly, and then it's all shot," she explained, laughing. She recognized that the reactive nature of the work was going to be a challenge—and it was, for her and for others in the study. Being responsible for handling a heavy and diverse array of tasks is one thing; maintaining the readiness to do so when it's difficult to predict what's coming next is another. It takes a toll.

Workdays filled with an ongoing stream of demands and unexpected and accompanying interruptions all contrive to consume principals' time. Add to that the burden of getting up to speed with changing rules and requirements in response to new district regulations or state policy changes and a national policy environment that is also in constant flux. Principals' time crunch is easy to understand.

## STRATEGIES FOR MANAGING TASKS AND TIME

Principals can navigate the tension between limitless tasks and limited time by employing various coping strategies—among them prioritizing tasks, protecting specific times, and embracing challenge. As principals gain experience in the role, they can continue to rely on and improve upon these strategies to help manage the day-to-day logistics of their work.

### Prioritize Tasks

Based on the rhythm of the school day, principals can find ways to manage the tasking time dilemma by purposefully constructing schedules that fit the demands of the job. "You just prioritize what you do during the day," Nathan explained. One way he coped was by shifting certain tasks to the early mornings and late evenings: "I can do reports at night; I can do reports at 4 in the morning when I get up. I don't need to do reports at the school." In the midst of her first year, Kathy described a similar approach, mentioning "those early mornings of getting on the e-mail to check what I need to address now and those late evenings of either just sitting and looking at e-mail or preparing for what needs to happen the next day." She added, "Some days I just stop and say, 'I'm not moving until I finish this.'" Kathy continued this strategy in her second year, explaining, "You don't want to do all that desk work when there are people in the building. Often I bring things home." Both Nathan and Kathy relied on the edges of their days to complete tasks that could be done privately without the interruptions that come throughout the regular school day. They also found time on the weekends or vacations to attend to tasks that required more sustained focus. Kathy and others in the study also periodically closed their office doors to take care of tasks that required confidentiality or more sustained and intensive concentration.

## Protect Specific Times

Although it's important for principals to be available throughout the day and responsive to various stakeholders, it's possible for them to protect small amounts of time in the midst of the bustle.

Principals in the study learned to schedule certain times of the day and certain days of the week for closed-door sessions and particular tasks, such as observing classroom instruction or meeting with parents. One way that Jennifer protected her time was by instituting a new process for parents to follow. If they had questions about their child's progress, they were to talk with the teacher first; if the issue was not resolved, only then would the parent bring it to Jennifer. Routines like this offer principals a way to structure their time and activities and impose some semblance of order to manage the unpredictability of their work.

Principals can also work to set boundaries around the work to preserve time for themselves and their families. This typically means identifying particular times and pursuing activities that are completely separate from their professional lives. Of course, even with their best efforts, there are certain times when they cannot ignore or avoid calls from work, and crises are not always confined to the regular work hours.

George, who described himself as a systematic thinker, endeavored to follow a plan in order to establish boundaries and reported some success with this strategy. Despite his efforts, though, the day-to-day demands of the position coupled with his sense of being ultimately responsible intruded constantly. "You can have the best plan for the week or the best plan that you know of at 7:30 in the morning, and then by 8:30, it's out the window. It's so hard not to get caught up in putting out fires," George explained. He reported having to constantly abandon daily and weekly plans, and he attributed this to the sense of ultimate responsibility he felt:

> It is different from when I was a teacher leader or even an assistant principal. Then, I knew that things didn't end at my door, so I did not have to be responsible for those and could stay focused on the planning and implementation of whatever I owned. But now, ultimately,

I own everything here. If something doesn't get taken care of some-where else, it comes to me and it ends at me.

The responsibility dilemma adds to the complexity of managing the task-ing time dilemma. Even so, principals rely on the strategy of prioritizing and planning despite the need to shift gears and abandon plans often. Perhaps the limits of the prioritization strategy explain why so many principals take a different tack, which we will look at next.

## Embrace the Challenge and Savor the Rush

Despite the work overload and stress that comes with managing tasks and time, many principals report loving their jobs. With ultimate responsibility comes a sense of fulfillment and meaning. Nathan noted, "I think it's the best job, really. It's so much better than being an AP." Kathy expressed similar senti-ments. Reflecting on her first five years on the job, she brought up how much she loves her role and how much she loves the community and the work she has committed to doing. She explained that some of the most satisfying days are the days when there is the most going on: "When there are a million things coming at me, in some ways, those are the days that I get the biggest rush out of." In a way, the quest for challenging work that draws so many to the prin-cipalship finds an answer in the ongoing management of task overload. It's a rush that principals find rewarding.

Reflecting on her first year on the job, Jennifer likened being a principal to "an adventure, because you never know what to expect. It's always thrilling, exciting, and engaging. It really is. I don't get a moment to sleep; I don't get a moment to sit down. That's what it's like—a nonstop adventure." Jennifer thrived on the excitement of ongoing challenge, even as she acknowledged that her planned work time was often interrupted by the unexpected. Then again, unpredictability is a key ingredient in any adventure.

Kathy summed up the situation when she noted that multitasking is cen-tral to the principal's role and part of what made the work thrilling for her. By embracing the energy that comes with juggling tasks and time, principals can reframe the unpredictability of the work as something to sustain their enthusiasm so that they thrive on the challenge. This enthusiasm helps to sustain them as they invest long hours in the work. Of course, embrace of this consuming work surfaces another dilemma for the principal—balancing work life and home life. Figuring out the calculus of fulfilling endless professional responsibilities while attending to personal and family obligations is a dilemma that principals continually strive to manage. We will talk more about this in the pages ahead.

Prioritizing and protecting particular times for work and embracing the challenges that come with the position are ways for principals to cope with the dilemmas associated with task overload and time shortage. By negotiating and renegotiating their schedules, setting boundaries around their work times, and connecting with the excitement they find in the position, they manage to make it work. At the same time, though, they must be careful that managing the tasking time does not infringe on their obligations to self and family. It is an ongoing struggle.

## Discussion Questions

1. *Reflection:* Kathy admitted continuing to struggle with time management even with several years of experience under her belt. Based on the strategies discussed and what you've learned about Kathy, what advice might you give her?

2. *Application:* We all struggle to find balance in our lives. What have you learned about your own work habits when it comes to managing tasks and time? What strategies have you relied on to juggle the various demands on your time? What works (and doesn't work) for you?

3. *Implications:* Given the challenge of limitless tasks and limited time, what structural changes might help new principals redefine their roles? What kinds of support from the district would help manage the tasking time dilemma?

# 5

# COOPERATION AND COORDINATION

"I can't do it all myself," Oscar concluded just a few months into his tenure as the principal of Tulip Elementary. He was right. The cooperation of others is essential to the work of the school principal. New principals soon realize that they cannot meet their educational ambitions for their schools single-handedly, nor can they expect to meet increasingly stringent and punitive performance metrics without schoolwide cooperation. Nathan, the new principal at Spruce and a former coach, compared the cooperation challenge he faced to getting his students and staff "on his team." A self-described people person, Nathan began his principalship with a plan to help those around him "identify their strengths and leverage those strengths to achieve the goals."

Coordination is also vital. Education is a collective endeavor, and it requires an organized approach from the staff, students, and even parents. Some degree of synchronization is crucial, whether the focus is on what students should learn from one grade to the next, which instructional practices staff will undertake, what constitutes misbehavior, and what the appropriate discipline is for various misbehaviors. When Jennifer started at Bur Oak, there were no structures in place to ensure instructional coordination within and across grade levels. She built them. For her, Nathan, and other new principals in the study, the challenge of obtaining cooperation and coordination began by first determining what was going on in their schools: doing diagnostic work to identify problems and then doing the design work necessary to transform the current reality into something better.

In this chapter, we describe the study principals' diagnostic and design work as they engaged with the twin challenges of cooperation and coordination, and we explore the approaches they used to motivate staff, develop staff capability, and get people to work together. We also look at how they managed the dilemma of balancing commitment and control that is common when school leaders enlist stakeholders to cooperate in a coordinated manner. We examine the related dilemmas that can surface—specifically, the challenge of balancing the need to differentiate among staff with the ideal of treating everyone equally and the pressure to demonstrate improvement while honoring the pace of securing cooperation. The chapter closes with three strategies principals can use as they navigate these dilemmas and work toward cooperation and coordination.

## LEARNING THE LAY OF THE LAND: DIAGNOSTIC WORK AND ITS CHALLENGES

"I'm like a doctor in some way," Alejandro explained. "I'm constantly seeing people, one after another after another. Some of my days are just spent talking to people. And sometimes I don't feel like they're productive, but you're a problem solver, you're a psychologist."

The medical metaphor Alejandro used is a fitting one. As we described in Chapter 1, like doctors, principals must work to define problems through diagnostic work and then craft solutions in an effort to ameliorate these problems. For new principals, the challenge is compounded by having to figure out how things work in their schools, how schooling is and has been done there, and who takes responsibility for which aspects of the work. "As a leader, you really need to be able to assess people's strengths well," explained Rich soon after he took the principal position at Sevenson Elementary. "Then you need to use that to make informed decisions about the right place for each person to be." Conducting their own investigative work is a way for new principals to identify what works and what needs fixing and then create a vision of what they want to achieve based on this diagnosis.

Initial diagnostic work is not easy, and it's more difficult still for principals who transition into the role from the outside and must simultaneously learn the school from scratch and establish themselves as leaders. At the end of her first year as Bur Oak's principal, Jennifer said, "I think the most challenging thing was not being informed and not having a real transition." For principals who are new to their schools, figuring out how things work, let alone what might account for any mediocrity, is extremely time-consuming.

Even prior to signing her principal contract, Jennifer conducted an informal survey of the staff at Bur Oak, asking them to identify things they thought needed attention during the upcoming school year, their concerns, and their ideas for engaging parents. As she explained in an interview, the former principal, her predecessor, "told a lot of wonderful stories, and then that was it. So I didn't know what state the school was actually in. I didn't know the strengths of the students, or the teachers, or the parents. I didn't know what resources were available to me. I had to figure everything out." Indeed, the previous principal at Bur Oak was apparently so intent that Jennifer get to know the school's staff on her own that she boxed up and stored all personnel files. Jennifer came upon them by chance in the counselor's office several months into her first year as principal. It was then that she figured out that staff who she had identified as having difficulty "had a history of past misconduct that was never really dealt with; they just got a written notice saying, 'This is my concern; I want you to handle it.' But no suspension, no nothing." Like a detective, Jennifer sought out and pieced together information about her staff. She spent a lot of time interviewing teachers, parents, and other stakeholders in order to figure out the lay of the land at Bur Oak.

Jennifer's diagnostic work turned up a number of surprises, including the lack of vertical and horizontal coordination in the curriculum and the weak enforcement of school rules on everything from parental involvement to employee conduct to student discipline. "Teachers had been run out of the building by the parents," she said. "Kids didn't have to wear their uniforms; they could do whatever they wanted to do." She also determined that, contrary to the previous principal's evaluations, the teaching staff were not "superior" teachers, although "some of them have the potential to be excellent."

She was particularly troubled by the lack of coordination between Bur Oak's classroom teachers and special education and bilingual teachers, which led her to issue this stinging verdict:

> If you don't collaborate with the special ed teacher, if you're not sensitive to bilingual students, and if you don't use strategies to help those students, you cannot be a superior teacher—I'm sorry. If you don't want to work with parents as partners in this learning, you're not a superior teacher.

For Jennifer, the biggest surprise was that there were no articulated standards or expectations for teachers, students, or parents. She acknowledged that most of her staff were "decent teachers," but she was troubled to learn that teachers at Bur Oak appeared to have never received formative feedback from school administrators on their lesson planning or on their classroom teaching. She also gained distressing insight into some teachers' attitudes toward Bur Oak's majority Hispanic student body. "I've got people in my building who are racially insensitive," Jennifer said bluntly. Although she had not intended to make a lot of changes in her first year, once she figured out what was going on at Bur Oak, it was clear to her that she needed to start shaking up "business as usual" right away.

Sevenson Elementary is located in a primarily Hispanic neighborhood, but the vast majority of its students are African American. Almost all of them qualify for free or reduced-price lunch. When Rich took over as principal, he spent his first few months gathering diagnostic data; like Jennifer, he was surprised by what he found. Despite low student performance outcomes, the staff at Sevenson mostly thought they were doing a great job. Many expressed hostility to the idea of change and blamed students and parents for the state of affairs at the school. Toward the end of his first year, Rich confided,

> It was surprising to me just the degree to which teachers can have a tremendously inflated sense of what they're doing. That led to some real struggles, with me saying, "OK, here's what I see. And here's where it's not acceptable.'" Some teachers just completely refused to accept that.

As the work of Cynthia Coburn (2006) reminds us, defining problems and challenges involves assigning blame; someone will always be implicated as the cause of the problem.[1] Problem definition can also upset people's sense of equilibrium. Rich struggled with how to work with teachers who honestly thought they were doing well until he arrived and told them otherwise. As he learned, doing diagnostic work as a newcomer and outsider is all the more challenging when the principal has to tell teachers and other staff that what they believe to be an acceptable performance is not good enough.

Diagnostic work is also challenging when the people with whom principals are working are not used to being asked for their opinions. Jennifer found that Bur Oak's teachers and parents were unaccustomed to having someone seek their input. No one had given them a survey before or invited them to participate in the school improvement process. While some were simply surprised to be asked their opinions, others were openly resistant. Jennifer was committed to engaging as many voices as possible in the process, but she recognized that she needed to strike a balance in her requests. She didn't want to push too hard, because she knew diagnostic work was just the first step in the complex work to come.

## TRANSFORMING THE LAY OF THE LAND: DESIGN WORK AND ITS CHALLENGES

Doing diagnostic work is an ongoing priority for principals, and it feeds into the related but different matter of doing something about any problems that come to light. Designing and implementing solutions is not something principals can do alone.

Instead, they must gain and maintain the cooperation of others, including staff, students, and parents, and they must also coordinate the efforts of these groups so that their work complements and supports one another. Principals must manage to gain the cooperation of others in a coordinated manner if they have any hope of resolving problems identified through their diagnostic

---

[1] Read Coburn (2006) for more information about how framing problems can shape social dynamics.

work. It's a matter of arousing will and developing skill, and it often requires a variety of approaches.

## Arousing Will

For principals, getting staff—especially teachers—to cooperate is continuous work. We can point to two reliable ways to gain the cooperation of others: securing commitment and establishing control.

*A commitment strategy.* Building a sense of commitment among staff to the school, to a vision for instruction, to ambitious learning outcomes, to the development of students, and to one another is often an effective way to elicit cooperation. The work involves creating a sense of community among stakeholders anchored in a joint endeavor by getting all staff to develop a sense of ownership. Improvement becomes "about us" rather than "about me." Many principals extend this strategy beyond the teaching staff. "I'm trying to really have everybody take ownership in the successes of the children," Jennifer reported. "You know—the grant leader, the after-school leaders, and also maintenance and security." By including everyone in planning meetings and making sure everyone had a voice in developing strategies for improvement, Jennifer hoped to build the necessary commitment to a common endeavor.

Many new principals find engaging others in their vision to be taxing because, more often than not, the staff they have is one they inherited rather than built. Gaining these staff members' cooperation in change initiatives is challenging in part because they may feel they are doing just fine. Comfortable in their routines and conditioned by prior administrations, they fail to see the need for improvement. For Rich, at Sevenson, this led to a struggle. He tried to remind people that they needed to do better, but this was an idea that some of his staff simply refused to accept.

New principals sometimes find that teachers' self-assessment of their practice and performance have been propped up by satisfactory or even superior evaluations from previous principals. Other times, staff feel they are doing the best they can and lay the blame for poor performance on the students and their families. Rich encountered both these responses at Sevenson. He was initially taken aback, but after a year on the job, he came around to recognizing how difficult it is to get people to see the need for change. Yet gaining cooperation for school improvement is difficult unless principals can convince teachers that improvement is necessary and that adjustments to their practice are a key component of such improvement.

Enlisting others' collaboration in the change process is one way to overcome their resistance. Jennifer found that having teachers investigate problems themselves built their commitment to solving those problems. She explained her approach: "I give the teachers time, I get substitute teachers, and I let them participate in walk-throughs. We have focus questions for the walk-throughs so it's not subjective, it's objective." By working together on both understanding and solving the problems, Jennifer and the Bur Oak teachers agreed on a focus area, initially homing in on mathematics. By engaging teachers in the process of defining the issues within that focus area, she laid the groundwork for getting their support in the design of the solutions and their commitment to implementation.

*A control strategy.* Sometimes a commitment strategy only gets principals so far in advancing their ambitions for their school, meaning it's necessary to try an alternate approach.

For some of the study principals, circumstances made relying on control seem necessary. After conducting meetings and observations and discussing the results of this diagnostic work during his first year as Sevenson's principal, Rich reported being surprised by

> the degree to which people, in the absence of really clear accountability and consequences, will do things that I consider to be completely unacceptable as professionals—whether that be being really negative and demeaning with students, even getting into physical discipline, or whether it be coming completely unprepared to teach.

He felt compelled to use the authority that comes with his position to press teachers to change their practice. This involved setting expectations and then monitoring teachers' progress toward those expectations to ensure they were met. He explained that his second year would be a time to move forward with clear directives for change and lay out non-negotiables for which all would be accountable.

Principals find establishing rules and setting expectations challenging in part because teachers are accustomed to operating on their own, mostly behind closed classroom doors. It can be difficult for principals to model behaviors for their staff and monitor practices closely enough to ensure expectations are being met. Rich's approach—keeping a close eye on how staff were working together and what they were doing in the classroom—was the only way he saw to hold them accountable, but such surveillance can make teachers and other staff uncomfortable, especially when they are used to operating relatively autonomously. Rich believed these steps were necessary to show how serious he was about the new direction he was setting for his school. At the end of his second year, he was happy to report that Sevenson staff had come to appreciate the consistency of vision and were confident that he was not going anywhere. He talked about the importance of both communicating and demonstrating that he meant business. The takeaway is that consistently and constantly enforcing expectations is essential to avoid the "this too shall pass" mentality among staff, which can lead some to simply wait out the change effort and go back to their old way of doing things.

## The Commitment and Control Dilemma

Although scholars often write as though commitment and control strategies operate in opposition, it's common for principals to use both strategies as they work on gaining the cooperation of their staff. It necessitates a delicate balancing act of managing what we call the *commitment and control dilemma*. If principals are too authoritarian, staff will resist. But if they never use control, they jeopardize the commitment of others, who may perceive them as lacking leadership. How much to emphasize commitment versus control depends on the situation.

Rich employed a commitment strategy to get his staff to buy into his vision and improvement approach but recognized a control strategy was necessary to get things done. A few months into the job, he confessed that one of his biggest fears had been "not wanting to come in with a hammer but still needing to [do so in order to] build in some real accountability." At this early stage of the game, he recognized the need to establish both commitment and control, and worried that he had left too many open questions about what might happen if teachers didn't commit to the change that he was asking them to embrace. As time passed, Rich became more adept at establishing control but continued to appreciate the tension between the two approaches.

To complicate matters, while a commitment strategy might work most of the time with most staff, principals may need to use the control strategy more directly with staff members who are reluctant to change. For example, some of Sevenson's teachers just didn't buy into Rich and his vision, leading to ongoing resistance. He acknowledged that his resulting, selective use of a control strategy led to another dilemma: treating staff differentially based on their levels of will and skill, while at the same time respecting the ideal of treating everyone the same. We call this the *egalitarian dilemma*. Principals struggle with the egalitarian dilemma, especially because teachers with whom they have to use a control strategy often feel they are being treated unfairly, singled out in ways that they consider to be unjustified. Perceptions of being unfair only add to the challenge of gaining cooperation.

## Developing Skill

Will and skill are intricately intertwined in principals' efforts to improve instruction. As described earlier, often the biggest challenge principals encounter in enabling improvement is staff who don't think improvement is necessary. And even when staff are on board and have the will to pursue improvement, there is the matter of designing an effective skill development program.

At the end of his first year, Rich argued that Sevenson's most important goal for the coming years was across-the-board improvement—for staff, for students, and for himself. He explained that his goal was not so much to hit a specific standard but to make positive progress. He explained, "It's about, did you grow this year? What made it happen? If you didn't grow, what could you have done differently, and what are the next steps?" For principals like Rich, helping teachers and other staff develop their knowledge and skills is central to improving the quality of teaching and learning in their schools.

Resistance to change among the Hoptree staff took new principal Alejandro by surprise. He was not discouraged, however. He took intentional steps to make his vision for improved instruction known to teachers, bringing it up during weekly faculty meetings and at regular grade-level meetings. Alejandro worked hard to make sure that teachers understood "that my number one priority from day one has been instruction, instruction, instruction." When he shared his expectations with teachers, he was careful to let them know that it's part of a teacher's job to grow and develop, just as it's part of a leader's job to grow as a leader.

Critically, Alejandro, like other principals in the study, recognized that simply expecting staff to grow was not enough. He had to foster that growth by identifying particular areas where improvement was needed. He set aside time for both one-on-one conversations with staff and opportunities for them to seek their own professional development. He said that, over time, he was "rewarded by seeing how people are evolving and changing and seeing the impact [he had] on them." In his view, developing instructional knowledge and skills in staff is what a good principal does. Alejandro explained that his role as an instructional leader was to ensure teachers had multiple opportunities to learn and improve their classroom skills.

Many principals in the study sought to extend development work beyond their staff and students to parents. Specifically, they wanted to provide opportunities for parents to learn and develop skills that would enable them to participate more actively in their children's education. Teachers at Bur Oak informed Jennifer that parents would not want to participate in academic activities because they would be embarrassed about their lack of education. Jennifer responded by asking staff to grapple with this issue rather than just accept it as a dead end. She asked, "How can we make parents feel confident in what they can do? How can we train them?" She shared examples of possible approaches she had seen implemented elsewhere, including holding workshops for parents throughout the school year so parents could learn how to better support learning at home, and organizing a family math night with all parents invited to come in and learn in small groups about how to do math at home with their children. Jennifer challenged her staff to come up with similar ideas that might suit Bur Oak's parent community, and by doing so she built schoolwide commitment to the work. Together, she and her staff introduced family science and mathematics nights to help parents explore the mathematics and science their children were learning at school.

Other principals' efforts to provide opportunities for parents to develop relevant skills were even more comprehensive in reach and ambitious in aim, and we will explore these in Chapter 7. Regardless of the focus, principals provided opportunities to develop skills as a key ingredient for securing staff cooperation in new activities.

## PURSUING COORDINATION

For principals, cooperation is essential, but so, too, is effective coordination of staff efforts.

When Jennifer started her job at Bur Oak, she assumed leadership of a group of teachers who were used to being autonomous. After a few months on the job, she had concluded that Bur Oak teachers pretty much did their own thing in their classrooms. At her school, as in many others, teaching was a cottage industry, not a collective practice. The lack of coordination went beyond just teachers' classroom practice. As Jennifer explained, "There were no universal expectations in the building with regard to anything—student behavior, student expectations, teacher expectations and performance, or parent involvement." Other principals in the study observed similar situations at their schools.

Shocked by the lack of coordination at Bur Oak, Jennifer set out to change things. At the most basic level, she knew setting clear expectations for teaching practice and student learning, including what content should be covered in each grade, was essential. Noting that the Bur Oak curriculum was a decade old, Jennifer engaged her staff in aligning the language arts, mathematics, and science curriculum both within and among grade levels. Next, Jennifer asked staff to let her know what resources they would need to implement the new aligned curriculum. She explained: "They had to look at an inventory—what they currently were working with, what they have—and then give me a list of all of the things they think we needed to purchase as a school to help facilitate this curriculum alignment." The changes were not easy, as they "upset structures that were already in place where teachers were allowed to order all their curricular materials." Still, Jennifer was excited about the newly coordinated instructional approach. She mentioned as an example the new science curriculum that extends from preschool through 9th grade. She said she could tell that the teachers were benefiting from "mirrored resources and mirrored strategies" at the different grade levels.

Jennifer's efforts to coordinate professional practice at Bur Oak went beyond aligning curriculum content and curricular materials. She also worked to standardize lesson plans, asking teachers not only to develop grade-level lesson plans but also to use the same format to ensure consistency. To support the implementation of this new practice, she made sure that the teachers had several samples to choose from and modify as needed. This emerged from work with teachers to identify formats that made the most sense for the school, followed by teachers meeting and deciding independently what lesson plan format Bur Oak should adopt. Jennifer explained that asking teachers to take leadership in this area was a way to build their commitment, and they would be held accountable for following the selected format. In this way, Jennifer linked the development of teacher cooperation to the coordination of her improvement efforts. She arranged for each to depend on the other.

Jennifer also worked with her staff to introduce ongoing progress monitoring for reading and math as part of Bur Oak's curriculum alignment process. For Jennifer, it was important not only to coordinate what content students would be exposed to within and among grades but also to coordinate curriculum, assessments, classroom work, and lesson plans. As she explained to her teachers, "You're saying you're doing these things, so I should see it in your lesson plans, I should see it in your assessments, I should see it in evidence of student work in your classroom." From Jennifer's perspective, such coordination was also the basis for collaboration among teachers about instruction and its improvement. It was intended to provide opportunities for teachers to reflect together on their practice, identify what was and wasn't working, and determine what next steps were needed. It allowed for ongoing diagnosis and coordinated improvements. Without a shared curriculum coordinated through common lesson plans and student assessments, such conversations about improving the quality of teaching would be difficult, if not impossible. In addition, Jennifer worked to coordinate professional practice at Bur Oak by providing common professional learning experiences for teachers and having teachers engage in regular and coordinated meetings with each other around the curriculum.

A core part of Jennifer's coordination efforts centered on ensuring that there were clear expectations for students consistently implemented across grades. When she arrived at Bur Oak, she was surprised to find that students "pretty much were allowed to poorly perform if they chose to do so. There were no consequences." Staff complained that students didn't turn in their homework and there was no support from administrators to get students to do their homework. So Jennifer and her staff developed a homework policy. More important, she worked diligently to ensure the policy was implemented by talking about homework daily with both students and teachers. She explained, "I check on them every day. And I say, 'OK, how's this group—6th grade—doing today with homework?'" Jennifer stressed to students (and their parents) the connection between doing homework and performing well, emphasizing students' power to make choices that would support their success. She told them, "This is a new year; you have a clean slate. You're either going to make it or break it based on the choices that you make." Jennifer's work in this area reminds us of the benefit of extending coordination efforts beyond professional staff to students and even parents. It also reminds us that a principal's coordination work depends on the commitment of all parties—and that it is by no means an easy endeavor.

## COORDINATION CHALLENGES

Coordination is difficult. Jennifer revealed that some staff at Bur Oak were resistant, or at least not initially well disposed, to working together in a coordinated manner. It is an understandable reaction, given they were accustomed to operating on their own, without coordinating with others. They wished to preserve the privacy of their professional practice. One lesson Jennifer learned about coordinating was how important it was to listen to staff concerns and better understand the reservations they had about her initiatives. Once she could grasp why staff felt the way they did, she was able to adjust the feedback she was giving them and clarify why things at Bur Oak had to change. Still, "getting feedback was a new thing for them," Jennifer explained, and she was mindful that her efforts would be counterproductive if the feedback she provided was too overwhelming and led staff to resist her coordination initiatives and undermine her efforts to build cooperation.

For many principals, Jennifer included, coordination work is complicated by increasingly punitive state and district policies that ask teachers to do more than ever before and that teachers perceive as infringing on their rights. Performance-based teacher evaluation, for example, makes it easier for administrators to fire teachers regardless of seniority. Jennifer reported that anxiety over job security was an obstacle to her coordination efforts, but she countered it by building an infrastructure to guide instruction and creating the conditions necessary for teachers to improve their own instruction by collaborating with one another.

Coordination was also challenging for Rich, who was confronted by staff unrest at Sevenson. He learned that teachers who were resistant to change and "refused to believe their practice was anything but great" nonetheless felt left out when they saw their colleagues working on teams to develop coordinated lessons plans and align the curriculum. They wrote off an embrace of Rich's coordination efforts as "seeking his favoritism."

The coordination and cooperation story at Hoptree involved Alejandro meeting with his Instructional Leadership Team weekly to discuss the school's improvement strategy for instruction and to make decisions related to instruction. He identified the leadership team as "the most gratifying part of my whole process here, because they're the heart and soul of the school in terms of the best and brightest teachers." In turn, decisions made by the leadership team were communicated and reinforced in weekly faculty meetings and grade-level meetings. As at Sevenson, though, staff who were not part of the team felt left out of the process. As we'll discuss in Chapter 6, depending on some to take leadership roles introduces the risk of alienating others.

Principals are challenged to find ways to be supportive and address the differentiated needs of their particular staff as they develop individuals' will and skill to change. At the same time, though, they have to further the coordinated development necessary for collective engagement in a shared practice, which is at odds with teaching's history as a cottage industry isolated in individual classrooms. As Jennifer explained, "The biggest thing you have to do is realize that educators can't perform or function in isolation." That is the cooperation and coordination challenge in a nutshell: principals work in schools where individual teacher autonomy and classroom isolation are still a dominant way of organizing for instruction, but they must depend on teachers working together toward shared goals if they are to have any chance of realizing their ambitions for their school. Further, parents must cooperate by ensuring their children show up to school regularly and on time and by encouraging their children to take their school work seriously. Students have to participate in classrooms, focus on learning, and do their homework. Most obviously, principals depend on school staff to work hard to improve students' opportunities to learn and coordinate this work within and across grades. Specifically, principals depend on the will and skill of their staff if they are ever to improve their students' opportunities to learn.

## STRATEGIES FOR MANAGING COOPERATION AND COORDINATION

As principals work to ensure cooperation and coordinate the work, they rely on several strategies to support others. They recognize both that change is a process, not an event, and that engaging others in the work over time is essential. They also develop infrastructure to support the process and differentiate their approach to persuade others to support their efforts.

### Coax Others Along

One strategy for gaining cooperation is to involve others in the change process from the outset. For principals, this means getting staff involved in shaping the process of change. By incorporating others in their decision making, principals can gradually build staffwide commitment and cooperation.

This kind of change doesn't happen overnight, meaning patience is essential. As Jennifer explained, "You have to keep in mind that the habits and routines that you want to change were not established overnight. It takes a long time to undo a habit." New habits and better-coordinated routines won't be achieved overnight, either.

The strategy of coaxing staff along does not just mean including them in discussions and meetings; it also means helping them master the skills they will need to do the work, which may include engaging in new activities, using new strategies, and participating in unfamiliar collaboration practices. By providing time for necessary professional learning, principals can develop staff capacity for cooperation and advance whole-school coordination.

Unfortunately, the gradual pace conducive to engaging others, gaining their cooperation, and developing their expertise is in tension with the urgency to demonstrate improvement. We call this the *urgency for results dilemma*. Principals' "success" often depends on showing demonstrable change quickly; district administrators demand it, and many parents expect it. What's more, improved results on valued metrics can also motivate staff and foster cooperation. At the same time, however, principals recognize that gaining cooperation from staff and other stakeholders is a long-term effort, and lasting change takes root through ongoing, leisurely practice. To balance the gradual pace of change with the urgency to demonstrate results, principals strive to show progress and create space to build cooperation and coordinate improvement efforts.

## Build Infrastructure

Efforts to coordinate instructional improvement are more likely to succeed if they are built on an infrastructure of a common curriculum, a common lesson planning approach, and common expectations and rules for students and staff. Principals can further support this infrastructure by building in time for teachers to work together on instructional improvement and setting up specific meeting times, schedules, and agendas to foster common planning opportunities for teams of teachers. Getting a new educational infrastructure operational requires time, effort, and constant monitoring by principals.

Three months into the job, Jennifer cited her daily visits to classrooms—something to which the Bur Oak staff were not accustomed—as an especially effective tool for ensuring the consistent implementation of new expectations and rules. She mentioned how she had begun reviewing samples of students' academic work and discussing it with teachers. Jennifer also instituted the practice of having groups of teachers work together to plan how to help struggling students. All these endeavors required a structure, a schedule, and a plan for how staff would work together. In Jennifer's view, having an educational infrastructure to support the work of teaching, maintain instructional quality, and lead instructional improvement was essential. This aligns with Jennifer's expressed ideal of shifting the principalship from a CEO model to a "master architect" one.

A solid infrastructure can help establish new habits and expectations in consistent and coordinated ways. It means that rather than being reactive or relying on haphazard strategies, principals carefully construct routines and procedures that foster coordination. By implementing these components one at a time and ensuring that they work well together, principals can build coordination to support ongoing instructional improvement.

## Differentiate Approaches

The same approach doesn't always work for everyone. Although a principal may set out with the goal to achieve cooperation and coordination, skill and will levels vary among staff—and among the broad population of stakeholders. Principals can and should work to develop cooperation by adjusting their approach, drawing on various commitment and control strategies depending on the individuals with whom they work. This is worth repeating: although being consistent is important, staff and stakeholder diversity means principals cannot rely on a uniform approach as they work to coordinate staff and other stakeholders and gain their cooperation.

Engaging in the twin challenges of cooperation and coordination means blending commitment and control strategies to provide tailored motivation and capacity development. It also means getting to know staff and stakeholders and strategically differentiating how to work effectively with these individuals.

These efforts to achieve cooperation and coordination within a school inevitably surface a number of dilemmas for principals to manage. Navigating the commitment and control dilemma is a leadership challenge that requires principals to strike a balance between being authoritative and authoritarian. To manage the urgency for results dilemma, they must balance pressure to quickly demonstrate improvement with the need to proceed at a pace that will enlist staff cooperation rather than undercut or deter it. Dealing with the egalitarian dilemma requires principals to balance the need to treat staff differently in order to effectively address their specific needs with the egalitarian ideal that permeates the schoolhouse.

## Discussion Questions

1. *Reflection:* When Alejandro arrived at Hoptree, he learned there were two distinct programs in place serving similar groups of students. How could he have coordinated the bilingual and general education programs? What strategies might he have used to gain cooperation from both sets of teachers?

2. *Application:* We all have different comfort levels when working with others. When it comes to gaining cooperation, are you more comfortable with a commitment approach or a control approach? How effective have these approaches been for you? Think of examples from your own experience leading initiatives.

3. *Implications:* Infrastructure for coordination varies widely in different schools. What structures might make sense to develop in schools to improve coordination? What might get in the way of those structures working?

# 6

# SHARING LEADERSHIP

By the end of her first year as a principal, Kathy had come to an important realization: "I don't have to do it all. And it doesn't always have to fall on the assistant principal, either. I can develop leadership amongst the teachers."

Although Kathy still felt ultimately responsible for Nyssa's success, she recognized that leadership didn't have to come from her alone. This is a common epiphany. The multiplicity of the principal's responsibilities, along with the wide range of expertise that must be mastered to fulfill those responsibilities, nudges many principals to involve others—not only to support their coordination efforts but also to participate in the central work of leading and managing the school.

Divvying up responsibility for various aspects of the job is one way that new principals endeavor to reduce the volume of the work and the diversity of tasks they have on their plates (see Chapter 2). To a certain extent, they do this simply by delegating—handing off discrete tasks to trusted staff and making sure the work is completed. But they can also take steps to share leadership with others, allowing those individuals to help make key decisions and carry the management load going forward.

While developing a more distributed leadership network provides some relief from the relentless pressure related to feeling ultimately responsible, it also adds to a principal's workload. As new principals learn to share leadership, they must devote substantial time and resources to building trusting relationships and determining and developing the capabilities of their staff. Sharing leadership also requires them to navigate the *responsibility dilemma*—finding ways to balance empowering others to lead with their own sense of ultimate responsibility. And they must confront (again) the *egalitarian dilemma*, which surfaces when some staff take on special responsibilities and others do not.

In this chapter, we explore the dilemmas associated with sharing responsibility and present a set of strategies principals can use to manage them and promote and support leadership among others: identifying allies, placing staff in roles that match their strengths, and gradually releasing control.

## SHARING LEADERSHIP, SHARING THE LOAD

Overwhelmed, Jennifer looked to others to help her cope with the workload. She needed to ease the stress she felt from taking on too much. Although she recognized there were some things that she, the principal, must do, she also saw ways others could help. "The success of our school is largely dependent upon the people in it," she explained. "It's not about the money or anything like that; it's about the people."

Jennifer went on to rely on those people—the Bur Oak staff—as an important resource. They helped her manage her responsibilities, but they also stepped up to help lead and manage the school. For Jennifer, sharing leadership was more than a way to cope with the demands of the job. It was also a way to build staff commitment to the school by enlisting them to take on different roles and help make decisions.

Even as Jennifer saw sharing leadership as a way to relieve some of the burdens of her work, she also appreciated it as a way to build support for her agenda. As she explained,

> I just try to let them see that I want them to be the leaders. I explain that it's easy to criticize [new initiatives], but if they don't involve themselves in any of the work, then how are they really contributing to the success of our school?

For principals, encouraging leadership among staff can be an effective way of engaging them in improvement efforts and securing their cooperation. Of course, this runs the risk of backfiring. A principal who empowers others may find these new leaders steering colleagues down a path different from the one originally intended. Managing the *responsibility dilemma* requires principals to enlist the talents and vision of others while still maintaining progress toward the original vision and goals.

Over time, Jennifer found that sharing leadership did help ease the demands of the job. Toward the end of her first year, she observed,

> My grade-level team leaders have been the most helpful. They are finally seeing themselves as teacher leaders, taking initiative with their colleagues and leading, not just in the classroom, but leading with a team. And that has been a big deal.

Jennifer invited teachers' input and ideas with new initiatives, asking questions like "How can we go about rolling this out into the building? What should our first step be?" From there, Bur Oak teachers developed and implemented action plans for a variety of content areas, such as reading, math, and science. In doing so, they built their skills as teacher leaders.

For principals, sharing leadership means more than asking staff members to complete specific tasks. It also means finding ways to empower staff members to take responsibility for task design and implementation. Alejandro, who was hesitant to let go of responsibilities, chose to limit shared leadership at Hoptree Elementary to a handful of lead teachers. He explained, "I like to be very hands-on, and when I feel comfortable enough to let go, then I let go." He shared the story of working closely with one lead teacher, who had taken responsibility for supporting a group of bilingual teachers. Together, they developed a plan for a series of meetings, informal observations, and feedback sessions, which she then implemented on her own. Alejandro was able to step aside and let this lead teacher do the work on her own, but only after he was sure that she would keep him informed about how the work was going through regular check-ins.

Although Jennifer had a strong commitment to the idea of sharing leadership with the teachers at Bur Oak, she, too, struggled to balance the responsibility dilemma: how much of the leadership role to let go and how much to hold on to. Toward the end of her first year as principal, she began allowing teachers to start running the faculty meetings. For her, this was a difficult transition. "It freaked me out to be more of a participant than the facilitator," she admitted. Jennifer gradually let go of her position of sole authority figure, but her way of coping with the responsibility dilemma was to monitor and maintain constant communication with those staff members she relied on to share leadership duties.

## INVESTING IN DISTRIBUTED LEADERSHIP

It isn't enough to just hand off tasks; if those tapped to do the work lack the necessary skills, such delegation can create even bigger issues. Developing staff members into leaders represents a demanding investment of time and energy. As Jennifer said at the end of her second year at Bur Oak, "I can have a strong team here, but I have to build it, because they haven't had one before. They've never seen it. For so long, they were uninformed and unempowered." This is a common phenomenon. Before principals can share decision-making responsibilities, they must first train other staff members to do leadership work. It is a long-term investment. Like any school-based reform, it can't be accomplished overnight.

Alejandro found the leadership development among the Hoptree staff to be one of the more rewarding aspects of the job. He explained that he saw himself as a role model for teachers interested in leadership and "as someone who creates a climate that promotes taking a leadership role." A year into the job, Alejandro shared an example of a lead teacher with whom he was working closely. He recognized her contributions as a team leader, but also emphasized that she would not have stepped up to take on the role without his support. "I don't think she would have just done it on her own, because I know she was always looking for affirmation. I did enough of that to guide her," Alejandro said. With his encouragement, she took on a leadership role and led an initiative to implement structured support for students who were struggling. Alejandro explained that her existing strong relationships with other teachers were a factor in the effort's success. They trusted her and were willing to use her new system in their classrooms with her guidance. Admittedly hesitant to share leadership at first, Alejandro began by identifying a few key individuals to share the leadership load with him and provided support for them over a period of time, during which he came to rely on them more and more. Ultimately, he demonstrated—to himself as much as to others—that sharing leadership was a way for him to achieve his vision for improving Hoptree.

Janice took another approach as she worked to develop her leadership team at Poplar Elementary. When she was promoted to the principalship, the school already had a leadership team in place. However, in Janice's view, the team lacked the expertise and structure necessary to fulfill the leadership responsibilities. So, rather than empower specific individuals, as Alejandro had done, Janice drew on training materials and protocols available through the district and provided the entire team with formal training to help them develop leadership skills and feel more comfortable in their leadership roles. Janice noted,

> At first, they were a little hesitant; nobody ever wanted to say anything about anybody because they were colleagues. They were not necessarily comfortable giving suggestions. But I think now they're really becoming true school leaders.

Janice's investment paid off relatively quickly. By the one-year mark of her principalship, she was already relying on the Poplar leadership team to help plan reform efforts and engage in essential tasks, such as hiring teachers.

With time, training, and support, school staff can learn to take on leadership roles and execute them well. The investment, although substantial, yields rewards for principals, who describe a sense of fulfillment that they derive from helping staff grow into leaders.

## CHALLENGES OF SHARING LEADERSHIP

While principals believe that investing in staff leadership development pays dividends, they often find that sharing leadership is challenging and easier said than done. What's more, once structures for sharing leadership are in place, they require ongoing attention to enact them consistently in practice. Because principals feel such a powerful sense of ultimate responsibility, managing the process of sharing leadership involves hard work and dedication over time. Negotiating the politics of sharing leadership can easily overwhelm them, as can the challenge of finding the resources to build and maintain structures to support others' leadership. As principals navigate these challenges, they encounter various dilemmas that emerge from engaging others in leadership.

## The Responsibility Dilemma Revisited

Principals' sense of ultimate responsibility can undercut their efforts to involve others in the work of leading and managing. At Nyssa, Kathy recognized that sharing leadership required her to empower others to take on work for which she was ultimately responsible. Still, she struggled with it. "That tendency to micromanage . . . I just felt like I had to keep that in check," Kathy explained at the end of her first year. She admitted that micromanaging had not been her style before she became a principal, but afterward, "I felt like I had to have my hand in all the different things going on." This is the responsibility dilemma in action: working to involve and share leadership duties with others yet feeling too pressed by the sense of ultimate responsibility to loosen the reins.

Janice confronted the responsibility dilemma as she sought ways to engage the Poplar staff in leadership. At the end of her first year, she explained that, although she had invested in her leadership team, she remained well aware of her own position as *the* school leader. This meant she had to strike a balance between responding to staff input and making the best decision from her vantage point, where she could see the big picture. Because Janice wanted Poplar to be the best it could be, and because she saw its ultimate success as a reflection on her, ceding any leadership responsibility was difficult. What if doing so jeopardized her vision and school improvement efforts?

Janice navigated the responsibility dilemma by constantly reminding herself that much of the pressure she felt was self-imposed. This was not entirely accurate, because the expectations of others do contribute to principals' sense of ultimate responsibility; indeed, it's not uncommon for principals' efforts to share leadership to be countered by policymakers' and parents' demands for principals to exercise their authority. Staff and parents often prefer to interact directly with the boss rather than with any surrogate. Principals must navigate these expectations from others as they manage the responsibility dilemma, adding to the challenge of sharing leadership with their staff.

## Playing Favorites

Building shared leadership invariably creates insiders and outsiders— those who are asked to assume leadership responsibilities and those who are not. For principals, this surfaces the *egalitarian dilemma* discussed in Chapter 5. They must balance the practical reality of treating some staff differently with the ideal of treating everyone the same.

To dispel perceptions that there was a privileged "in group" of Hoptree staff, Alejandro initially tried to carry the leadership load on his own. As he explained, "I was fighting against the perception of playing favorites so much because I knew it was viewed in such a negative way here." However, he quickly realized that he needed to involve other staff at Hoptree in the leadership work. He reached out to a handful of teachers with whom he had developed strong relationships and asked them to take on leadership responsibilities. While Alejandro still had to manage the egalitarian dilemma, he gradually relied on others to help him lead.

Janice also tried to avoid creating an inner circle, or "chosen few," out of concern that doing so would blunt her efforts to distribute responsibility. By making leadership opportunities inclusive and open to all, she managed to interest more of her staff in the leadership work at Poplar. She expanded the school leadership team to include roughly a third of staff and joked that soon it would include the entire staff. While recognizing the value of such an engaged staff, Janice also acknowledged that this inclusive leadership approach has its limitations—among them, the difficulty of addressing issues efficiently in such a large group. Her efforts to balance the need to be inclusive with empowering a few key leaders resulted in a cumbersome structure that sometimes encumbered decision making.

Kathy faced a similar concern at Nyssa. She explained, "There are a lot of people on staff that would fit the criteria to be on the leadership team, but I can't have a committee of a whole because then it defeats the purpose." Her solution was to limit leadership team membership to two-year terms and rotate staff on and off the team. This structural adjustment helped offset the perception that she was playing favorites, but only to a degree. At the end of her second year, Kathy had come to this conclusion:

> I think there are a lot Type A personalities here. They think the leadership team has a certain cachet—that those who are on it are favored in my mind. And I didn't realize that. So I talked to the team about it, and next year, we're going be much more formalized in their reporting out to different committees about what is going on.

By creating additional and more transparent procedures, Kathy hoped to quash perceptions of favoritism. It's worth noting that this took time and energy and potentially undermined the efficiencies Nyssa gained from sharing leadership.

Empowering others to engage in leadership has the potential to lessen the leadership load for principals *and* build commitment among staff, but at the same time it has the potential to alienate those who are not chosen. Even principals who strive to be fair cannot avoid relying on some staff more than others. Building trust is a vital tool in managing the resulting egalitarian dilemma—both trust with those who participate in the shared leadership and trust with other staff who may feel left out of decision making.

## Building and Maintaining Trust

Principals' initial reluctance to empower their staff is often driven by a lack of trust. Typically, they are concerned that the actions of staff with whom they share leadership will reflect poorly on them or that it will lead or contribute to other problems. In short, they worry that efforts to share leadership would increase their burden rather than help to alleviate it.

For Alejandro, issues of trust came up early in his transition to the principal's office. Struggling with the transparency dilemma (see Chapter 3), he had trouble navigating what information he could share and what he ought to keep confidential. This led him to be overly cautious about confiding in members of his staff. "I guess I'm a little bit more guarded," Alejandro confessed. "It's a terrible feeling when you feel like you have to filter yourself."

Although Kathy was committed to empowering the staff at Nyssa, throughout her first year, she struggled to trust their input on decisions. She had heeded her assistant principal's suggestion to assemble a leadership team with diverse views and appreciated the resulting perspectives. The complication was that many of the leadership team's perspectives challenged her own vision for improvement. By the end of the year, she had come to a new understanding:

> I think we learned from each other, and the experience gave me insight into where they're coming from. It raised my level of respect for them. It was a struggle, though, because we weren't on the same page on a lot of things. My hope was that by working with this group and giving them some leadership, they would just all come along downstream with me. And it didn't work so much. They're still the same people they always were. And really, how arrogant of me to think that I was going to change who they are as people.

In her second year, Kathy was more selective when putting the leadership team together. She was careful to include teachers who were more aligned with her own instructional vision. All principals must identify when it is wise to reach out to those with different ideas and when it is wiser to focus on empowering those most supportive of their improvement agenda.

Trust is a two-way street. As Janice explained, it took time for her staff to learn to trust her commitment to empowering them as teacher leaders. "Once they saw that their opinions really were taken into consideration and mattered, I think they started to become more and more comfortable," Janice said. The authentic experience of sharing leadership helped her realize that trusting her staff was an important step toward having them trust her.

Caution is required. Some aspects of sharing responsibility, such as being perceived as playing favorites or asserting positional authority when others make decisions that don't align with the established agenda, can undermine trust and detract from cooperation, both of which can be enough to derail improvement efforts. Principals encountering these issues are advised to consider compromise. Sharing leadership often means adapting the initial plan to incorporate the ideas of others and, sometimes, changing it to be something that will garner more support and cooperation and thus have a better chance of success.

## Time and Money

Principals can and do identify ways to share leadership, but time and money are essential resources for supporting these efforts. This presents a challenge, given the reality of limited funding and the shifting priorities of central offices.

Like many principals, Jennifer recognized that the primary cost associated with sharing leadership with her staff was time. At the end of her first year, she explained that efforts to create a leadership team had started off well, but as the demands of the school year increased, staff struggled to find time to meet. In school settings, time definitely means money. Jennifer had to seek and secure funding to compensate her leaders for time spent planning outside the contract day. She explained,

> I'm hoping the district extends the school day, honestly, because we just don't have enough time to do any work. I mean, it is *so* rushed. So even if we had another 45 minutes, it would be a big help. We need to have more dedicated time toward the practice.

The reality is that the time and money so essential to building strong shared leadership are rarely guaranteed. Although Jennifer was able to secure additional pay for teachers who took on leadership responsibilities, the budget shifted during the summer prior to her second year, leaving her with fewer resources than anticipated. "We used to have a fund of $20,000 for the instructional leadership team to meet and plan after school hours or weekends or Saturday, and it was wiped out," she said. "Teachers had done all this work in the summer and couldn't get paid."

## STRATEGIES TO SUPPORT SHARING LEADERSHIP

As new principals establish themselves in their leadership role, they can rely on a few key strategies to manage their efforts to share leadership. By identifying allies who share their vision, sharing responsibility in purposeful ways to ensure the right people are in the right roles, and gradually releasing control, they are better able share leadership and manage the dilemmas that arise as they empower others.

### Identify and Enlist Allies

Principals rely on their allies—often their assistant principals or key teacher leaders—to help them figure out whom to trust, how to share responsibility, and whom to empower as leaders. Kathy found an immediate ally in her assistant principal, who helped her negotiate many challenges that arose during her first year. At the end of that year, she was full of praise for him, pointing out what a huge help he had been. "I think we're seen as a team," Kathy said. "The teachers and staff and families recognize that he has my trust and that when he speaks, he speaks for both of us. We're a united front." Recognizing she and the assistant principal had similar goals, Kathy not only found ways to share responsibility with him but came to trust him to accurately communicate her vision in his interactions with various stakeholders.

Alejandro also learned to rely on a handful of key allies; he even attributed his successes to these relationships. Still, he worried about excluding and alienating other staff members. Similar to Kathy, he recognized that sharing leadership is in part about managing the expectations of others, and he worked to help the rest of the staff understand his reasoning for relying on a few of them to help him lead. Alejandro's hope was that by maintaining his openness with the rest of faculty and ensuring that everyone understood they were welcome to come directly to him, no one would feel excluded. Finding the balance between relying on allies and maintaining the transparency necessary to keep everyone else engaged is crucial for working with the staff as a whole and managing the egalitarian dilemma. Through transparency and the trust that it builds, principals can mitigate the challenges emerging from sharing leadership with allies and not detract from efforts to gain broad cooperation from staff.

## Place the Right People in the Right Roles

Leveraging shared leadership involves empowering individuals with the necessary capabilities to take on particular responsibilities. At the end of her second year, Jennifer believed her strategy for constructing leadership teams had worked, and she was confident that everybody was where they needed to be. She had developed teams that drew on the strengths of individuals, putting people together who not only could collaborate with one another but also would complement one another's skills. She noted that team members "collaborate all the time. They even work on the weekends and go out to dinner. They enjoy what they do together, and they enjoy sharing experiences." Jennifer was proud of the dynamics that had evolved in Bur Oak's leadership team.

For Jennifer, the strategy of identifying individuals with the right skill sets and dispositions was key. She considered people's personalities and their technical skills. She explained,

> The ones who are really organized, I have to split them out amongst my teams so everybody is balanced out by their skill sets, between operational or even hidden talents that we might not have known about. Everybody has something.

Recognizing distinct skills, carefully considering the composition of teams, and shrewdly matching teams and tasks enabled Jennifer to build on the strengths of her staff. A valuable takeaway is that when distributing leadership, expertise is not just an individual consideration—it is also a collective matter, generated by different staff members in combination. Getting the right people in the right places requires thinking about which assembly of staff makes the most sense given their different skills.

While Kathy had challenges with her leadership team, by the end of her first year, she was confident that she had figured out the teachers she needed to empower in order to achieve her vision for improving instruction at Nyssa. For Kathy, data use was a central skill for team members to have. She explained:

> We were able to identify at each level key teacher leaders who were using data effectively, and we found opportunities for these teachers to work in teams and share with one another their data and different ways they can use their data.

Kathy attributed the rise in Nyssa's test scores to partnering teachers with different skill sets. Although many of her teachers were not experts on data, she identified those who were and strategically placed them in leadership positions so they could share their data use expertise with others. By thinking carefully about teacher leaders at each level and within each team, she was able to position teacher leaders strategically to distribute their expertise across teams. Like Jennifer, Kathy thought about expertise less as an individual quality than as a collective one.

Putting the right people in the right roles requires getting to know the capabilities of individual staff well. As principals enter their new positions, they should work closely with staff to learn their strengths, weaknesses, and aspirations for growth. Even in schools where leadership teams are already in place, every new principal must establish and communicate his or her own shared leadership model with its various roles and responsibilities to ensure that the individuals in those roles are well-suited to the work. Over time, as principals build stronger relationships with staff, they tend to rely more and more on staff expertise and leadership.

## Gradually Release Control

Scaffolding shared leadership is another way for principals to manage the responsibility dilemma. It's a strategy that allows them to provide support and maintain control until they trust that leadership activities can be enacted competently by others.

At first, Alejandro maintained tight control over leadership team meetings at Hoptree. In his first year, he wrote the meeting agendas and led the meetings himself to ensure they ran smoothly. As he put it, "I don't like to miss those opportunities to impress upon the team my vision and my goals." But planning for the second year, he envisioned a more active role for the leadership team—one that would parallel the greater responsibility they would be taking on to design professional development goals and support other teachers' efforts to pursue those goals in classrooms throughout the school. These were originally activities Alejandro imagined doing on his own. At the end of his third year, he was even more comfortable sharing leadership, and he expanded the leadership team to include additional members who would be responsible for leading for literacy improvement.

Similarly, Janice initially oversaw all aspects of the leadership team meetings at Poplar before gradually stepping aside and giving team members more autonomy and greater responsibility. In her second year, she invited the team to help with hiring, including them in reviewing résumés and enlisting them to serve on interview committees. She recognized that sharing leadership represented quite a culture shift for Poplar staff. As she put it, "These types of things have never been asked of them before, and I think now they're getting more comfortable taking more of a leadership role." She expressed hope that her gradual move to a shared leadership model would help the leadership team recognize how valuable it is to have a voice in key school decisions. But she also commented on how important it was to provide the leadership team with ongoing training to equip them to succeed in the new teacher leadership roles she was creating for them.

An important aspect of Janice's gradual release of control was her commitment to accountability. For Janice, greater input required greater accountability. Even as Poplar's teacher leaders took on more responsibility, she maintained the requirement that they report directly to her. It's a reminder that in order to manage the responsibility dilemma, principals must balance the release of control with holding teacher leaders accountable for getting the job done and done right.

Principals who share leadership through scaffolding, modeling, and monitoring the leadership work of others and then gradually allow these new leaders to take charge of and be accountable for various responsibilities do more than develop the leadership capabilities of their staff. They also build trust and establish the infrastructure that will support more effective shared leadership in the future, enhancing collaboration and coordination. Recognizing the need to foster leadership among others, these principals take time to identify allies, share responsibility in ways that ensure the right people are in the right roles, and gradually release control.

Sharing leadership is a complicated challenge. It requires principals to invest in others, ensuring these individuals have the support and resources they need to develop as leaders, and it surfaces a number of dilemmas that must be managed. Extending responsibilities to some staff but not others gives rise to the egalitarian dilemma, which can be navigated by building trust and managing expectations. The responsibility dilemma can be navigated by gradually releasing control only after staff have been thoroughly trained. Although sharing leadership with others is difficult, principals learn that it is crucial for managing the multiplicity of responsibilities their position requires. What's more, trusting staff helps staff trust their principals and builds commitment to their shared work.

## Discussion Questions

1. *Reflection:* Jennifer described the challenge of finding funding and time for staff to conduct their work. What kinds of strategies might she use to find time during the contract day for teachers to conduct leadership work, even when she can't identify stipends for their work outside school?

2. *Application:* We all need allies in order to get our work done, and sometimes we find them in surprising places. What strategies have you used to identify allies in your workplace?

3. *Implications:* Many of the new principals described in this chapter provided support to teachers as they engaged in leadership activities for the first time. How can principals strengthen leadership teams and improve their effectiveness? What kinds of development and support would be helpful?

# 7

# CREATING A SAFE SPACE

According to Octavio, a Spanish-speaking immigrant who became the principal of the majority-Hispanic Dogwood Elementary, the position entails much more than just instructional leadership. As he explained, he was committed to "developing a connection with children and providing for them the best of what we can do." Safety was a top priority for Octavio. Like many of the principals in the study, he focused on ensuring not only a physically safe environment but also a culture in which students felt safe enough to take risks in pursuit of meaningful learning. This is work that requires principals to contend with numerous social and political issues facing school communities and the surrounding neighborhoods.

Consider how issues like poverty, high mobility, and gang violence can disrupt not only the lives of students but also the day-to-day operations of a school. In many schools (particularly urban schools, like the ones in the study), there are also long-standing structural inequalities to consider, which may manifest as neighborhoods with fewer employment opportunities, limited access to resources (such as healthy food and civic organizations), and contentious relationships with police.[1] Obviously, the effects will differ from school to school, but these are challenges that all principals must learn to navigate in some form or another.

---

[1] Galindo, Sanders, and Abel (2017) provide more detail about how low-income schools are impacted by these structural inequalities and how some schools work to overcome them.

Principals like Octavio prioritize safety within the school by working to create spaces where students feel welcome and cared for, have the freedom to focus on learning, and can rely on teachers and staff to provide some stability for them regardless of their home and neighborhood circumstances. The logistics of this can be very complicated. While trying to establish positive conditions for learning and teaching inside the school, principals must figure out how to serve as a buffer and keep negative external factors at bay. Yet if they hope to maximize students' opportunities to learn and develop, they must find ways to connect with parents and other community stakeholders. This is what we call the *buffering and bridging dilemma*—the balancing act principals do to draw boundaries around the school to create a safe learning environment while simultaneously building bridges to the community to create a richer learning experience. In this chapter, we explore this dilemma, additional dilemmas that stem from it, and the strategies principals can use to navigate them.

## BUFFERING THE SCHOOL FROM OUTSIDE FORCES

Principals are challenged to build strong, supportive communities within the school where students and staff feel cared for holistically. As they focus on creating conditions conducive to learning within their schools, principals emphasize the need to create "safe spaces" for students whose lives outside school may be challenging due to economic or family instability, experiences with trauma, and limited access to social services. Although the term *safe space* has come to mean many things in education, we use the term here as principals tend to use it: as a way to describe the general condition of a calm, productive, and supportive environment where students have their basic needs met and do not need to worry about their physical or emotional safety. For some principals, this means feeding kids who haven't had breakfast; for others, it means setting up clothing drives to make sure all students have warm winter clothes. Still others focus on providing socioemotional support for students, such as mental health resources.

Safe spaces are characterized by a feeling of community. At Tulip Elementary, Oscar's first priority was ensuring that everyone working there "understands that we are a group of people who are working toward the same goals, helping each other, contributing, sharing our talents." Oscar recognized that the staff needed to feel that they were part of a broader mission extending beyond academic support, and he brought them together around the shared goal of supporting students' well-being. This focus on creating a collegial environment for staff with a shared commitment to support one another was Oscar's way to help establish community within the building—a community that could help buffer students from the challenges they faced in their economically disadvantaged neighborhoods.

In the midst of her first year at Sweetgum, Samantha came to understand that safety and stability went hand in hand with learning. As a new principal in a new school, Samantha and her staff faced a number of challenges as they tried to create a safe learning environment. She admitted being surprised by the level of need she saw in her students:

> Our take is that we're going to do whatever it is we have to do to meet their needs, but it's clear that those needs are significant. For example, in 2nd grade, we've got this cluster of students where we think, "Wow—how can we have this many who need this kind of social work?"

Given the shrinking safety net in the high-poverty neighborhoods where most of Sweetgum's students live and insufficient social work resources at the school, Samantha and her staff were left to do the best they could, and they were determined to do just that.

Although Sweetgum draws students from various parts of Chicago, the majority of its students come from low-income families. As she got to know these families, Samantha learned that many of them had changed schools many times—due to poverty-linked transience but also, she believed, due to other schools' inability to ensure safe spaces for these youth. She explained, "I think they've gone from school to school to school, partially because they felt like the school wasn't being responsive enough." She concluded that additional support was essential to address the issues Sweetgum's students were facing. For Samantha, prioritizing safety within the school meant identifying ways to support emotional well-being—no small task when social services are limited.

Part of Samantha's way forward was to hire new staff in the middle of her first year. She explained,

We really spent a lot of time interviewing, and what we were looking for was people who were willing to say, "These are the kids that we have, these are their needs, and we're going to get together and do whatever it is we have to do to meet their needs."

Samantha pointed out that students at Sweetgum faced a range of challenges in their lives, not just due to instability but, in many cases, due to violence. Behavioral issues were common. It made the task of ensuring a safe, nurturing environment all the more complex.

Over time, Samantha's efforts paid off. Reflecting at the end of her sixth year at Sweetgum, she shared how students would stop in during the summer months just to say hello. "They run up to the door to come speak to us all the time," she noted. "As much as they want to be on summer vacation, they also want to be at the school." Samantha also said that while she ultimately feels like she has succeeded in fostering a safe learning environment for students, she and others at Sweetgum must continue to cope with various outside disruptions that affect the teaching and learning that go on inside.

## BUILDING BRIDGES BEYOND THE SCHOOLYARD

City principals like those in the study typically enter their positions with plenty of experience working in low-income neighborhoods. However, the principalship brings new responsibilities and new opportunities to engage with the surrounding community. Principals are also ultimately responsible for managing expectations from external stakeholders, such as local neighborhood groups, and in a position where they might address some of the community's concerns.

As a new principal, Alejandro felt unprepared for the community-focused, "bridge-building" aspect of the position. He admitted to being taken aback by how quickly Hoptree's neighbors reached out to him for support. For example, he had only been in the job for a few months when a community group asked him to take up the issue of a house close to the school that a neighborhood gang was using. The issue had not directly affected safety within Hoptree, but Alejandro, worried about the students on their walks to and from school, spoke with the police about his and the community's concerns. He concluded that it was his responsibility to enlist the police as external allies who could help ensure a safe school environment. Although he acknowledged that engaging with the external community was necessary, he nevertheless worried about the additional time and energy it would require and how that might infringe on his ability to meet his primary responsibility to Hoptree's students.

For example, Alejandro explained that although he understood that the larger community thought he should be doing more to help clean up the neighborhood surrounding the school, he was perplexed about what he could actually do. "Do they really expect a principal to take care of a gang problem that even the police can't figure out how to resolve?" he asked. Though often unsure how to respond, Alejandro grew to appreciate how issues outside the school, such as the presence of gangs, had the potential to negatively impact the work inside the school and threaten the safe space they were trying to create. This is the buffering and bridging dilemma in a nutshell: the principal works to buffer a school from some negative aspects of life in the neighborhood, but in order to successfully protect children from external threats and create a safe space for learning, the principal must also reach outside the school and engage with the broader community, including neighborhood organizations and the local police.

Samantha worried that her staff at Sweetgum sometimes focused too much on what students faced outside school—instability at home, absent or disengaged parents, even a lack of healthcare—and too little on their academic experiences in the classroom. "We can't fix what's going on at home," she said, "but what we can do is equip these kids with skills. We can point out to them, 'You're a solid reader. You can do math, you can think, you can problem solve.'" She explained that her ongoing goal was to create supportive learning environments within the school where teachers focus on helping students build the academic skills that will prepare them for the future.

This is a good example of a closely related challenge—what we refer to as the *learning goal dilemma*. On the one hand, Samantha valued a focus on academic learning and emphasized boosting student achievement as a key goal for her teachers; indeed, this is the goal for which she and her school would be held accountable. On the other hand, she recognized the need to address socioemotional concerns in order to create a safe and positive learning environment. She hated to take time away from academics to address student well-being, but she also realized that unaddressed socioemotional needs could keep students from meeting academic goals.

For Samantha, managing the learning goals dilemma required her to engage with the buffering and bridging dilemma. By the end of her second year, she had reached out to various community partners to help address students' socioemotional needs. Sweetgum partnered with an arts association to offer an after-school program that provided art experiences that many students would not otherwise have been able to access. The school partnered with the city's parks department to make sure students had recreational opportunities, including athletics, outside school. A healthcare initiative brought medical services such as flu shots and diabetes screenings into the school and made them accessible during the school day. Whereas Alejandro was drawn out by community partners, Samantha actively reached out to build bridges to the external community and acquire services that would help her achieve her goals for Sweetgum. Through bridging, she buffered her staff from instability in the external environment and allowed them to focus on teaching and learning— which she also believed to be the best way to support students in the long run.

## PARTNERING WITH PARENTS

Families can be crucial connections to the community and a resource that principals can leverage to attain the school's goals. Samantha observed,

> Some kids come to school already equipped to do well no matter what teacher they have, and that's because someone at home reads to them. Their first teacher, the one at home, is doing their job. If we don't get those first teachers—parents—to do their job, then we're fighting even more of an uphill battle.

As is evident here, Samantha envisioned a particular role for parents: vital partners in creating a supportive learning environment within Sweetgum. She explained that she set out to engage families who did not have a history of involvement in their children's academic process.

At the beginning of her first year, Samantha recognized how challenging achieving this goal would be. She described some parents who "have battled me, and their attitudes were nasty. They didn't get how important school was." But she was undeterred and took the time to work with them and other parents over the course of the first year to lay the groundwork for effective partnership. At the end of her first year, Samantha was proud to reveal that she would be working closely with parents on a plan to extend learning into the home. She explained:

> We couldn't just say to parents, "We'll teach [your children] every-thing." Because we need kids to do their homework at home, we need them to read 30 minutes a night, and we need parents' support for this.

Just before the end of her first year, Samantha hosted a workshop for parents during which they met their children's next-year teachers, received a packet of summer materials, and talked with teachers about what kinds of learning activities families could facilitate at home. Her hope was that this kind of direct communication and explicit advice would help families identify ways to support their children's learning outside school—and thus bolster their children's learning in school as well.

Creating parent partnerships is not easy. Samantha actually expressed surprise at her early success, including the high attendance at the parent workshop she hosted. "It was raining, pouring buckets, and we had 200 parents in there," she noted. "The whole room was full. Everybody." She attributes the high turnout to the work done during the year to proactively reach out to families. How seriously she took parent partnership was reflected in the time she invested in enlisting parent support.

For new principals, learning about how families view the school is a necessary first step. This means reaching out and asking parents about their experiences.[2] Oscar, in his first year as Tulip's principal, learned through his conversations with families that many had felt excluded by his predecessor. "The families really want me to be more understanding than the previous administrator," he said. "They want me to be more accepting, to allow them to participate more, to honor their culture." As a Hispanic leader serving a primarily Hispanic community, Oscar felt that his ethnic and cultural background helped him build partnerships with families. At the beginning of his first year, he said this:

> I identify with many parents a lot, and I know what they want. We Hispanics have a certain way of treating people. We have a lot of respect for authority figures, for teachers. And when we feel that a person is not reciprocating that respect, we feel that there's a certain wall. I want to break down that wall. I want to make sure that people feel that they can come to me, and when they do, they will be respected, they're going to be listened to.

Oscar's efforts to bring families into the school was both personal and professional. Over time, these efforts paid off. At the end of his sixth year, he explained, "Tulip used to be pretty isolated from the community, and I changed that. I brought parents into the school and the classrooms and made them feel like a part of the school community." One of Oscar's achievements was creating a parent mentor program to train some parents how to support other families in the school community. It uses workshops to teach volunteer parents about school policies, how to communicate with the school, and how

---

[2] See Epstein et al. (2018) for more information about the importance of two-way communication. Too often, schools focus on delivering information from the school to the families, without attending to what schools can learn from families.

to get involved with their children's learning. Equipped with this knowledge, they passed it on and helped other families feel more comfortable engaging with the school. Oscar acknowledged that at first, the mentor program was a culture shock for many parents who were not used to participating in that way. He also had to overcome some parents' distrust of the school—a holdover from their interactions with the previous principal.

These efforts to engage parents as partners can exacerbate the buffering and bridging dilemma principals face. As we discussed in earlier chapters, some principals struggle to establish boundaries and keep parents out of the classrooms; however, partnering with parents often supports students' learning both at home and at school. For Oscar, the benefits of working with families outweighed the drawbacks. Indeed, he viewed building connections with families as a way to support students' learning at home and in school as part of his social obligation. Oscar explained that when parents become allies rather than outsiders, they can reinforce expectations for learning with their children. At the same time, he acknowledged, parents can make demands on leaders' time and attention, diverting them from a focus on student learning within the school.

It's worth noting that efforts to partner with parents seem to require less energy over time. Oscar found there was a certain momentum to family engagement. First, he clarified the plan to make a cultural shift from excluding parents to including them. Then, after the parent mentor program was established, he drew on these existing connections to build relationships with new parents and community members. In his case, Oscar's background and identity helped develop the initial trust and relationships that led to stronger partnerships with families at Tulip. Once those first relationships were forged, parents helped other parents learn about the school, expanding partnerships that deepened and grew with time.

## BUILDING BRIDGES TO OTHER SOURCES OF SUPPORT

Principals working to create safe spaces for their students at school can also enlist support from outside sources beyond family.

Nelson, whose school was in a high-poverty neighborhood that had been coping with gang activity, worked closely with the state department of Children and Family Services (CFS). Together, they identified the needs of particular students at Birch and linked up with various local agencies to surround them with additional mental health support and sponsor after-school activities. Nelson pointed out that the partnership with CFS only came into being "because of me screaming and yelling!" At the end of his first year, his efforts were already paying off in the form of increased attendance and fewer misconduct reports. Nelson was grateful for how the CFS partnership opened doors that allowed Birch to receive support from other agencies. "We rely on their wraparound service. You just identify what the issues are, and then they work with all the sister agencies to surround [students] with support," he explained. By inviting partnerships with these external agencies, Nelson found ways to provide his students with mental and physical health support that they might not otherwise be able to access.

Bridging to external resources helped Nelson work toward developing a safe, supportive environment within Birch to address students' socioemotional needs and manage the learning goals dilemma. Identifying and accessing relevant services from outside the school help principals create the conditions that allow students to focus on academics while they are at school. In general, partnering with public agencies and community organizations helps bring resources into schools where resources are lacking and provides students much-needed access to services that can be difficult for families to locate, afford, and schedule.

The city principals in the study also worked to build bridges with local law enforcement. For some of them, ensuring the basic safety of students required the involvement of the police. As Alejandro described, sometimes criminal activity in the neighborhood can threaten student safety on the way to and from school, and even at the school itself. Because of this, many principals focused on strengthening their relationships with police to help maintain the security of their schools. Samantha explained, "We had gone to visit the police commander to build a relationship. We ended up getting a police car that parked outside the school every day at 3 o'clock during dismissal and then after school at 5 o'clock. It was fantastic." From Samantha's perspective, the security that law enforcement provided in the near vicinity of the school helped to establish a sense of safety within the school.

It's important to note that outreach to the police is not without its challenges. After all, for some families who have had negative experiences with the police, law enforcement represents more threat than support. Recognizing this, Samantha highlighted that for Sweetgum's partnership with the police to work, she and other staff had to foster personal relationships between specific officers and the school community. Initially, Samantha developed this relationship herself by visiting the officers, sending e-mails, and "making friends with them." As she got to know individual officers, she invited them to visit the school and get to know the staff and students. At the end of her first year, Samantha said that the individual officers she worked with had become integral members of the community, known and trusted by students and families as allies. She viewed them as partners in creating safety at Sweetgum. Recognizing that this partnership relied on relationships with individual officers, she expressed hope that those particular officers would continue to work as liaisons between the school and law enforcement.

As principals grapple with the buffering and bridging dilemma, they come to recognize that buffering alone cannot ensure the physical and socioemotional safety of students. Given the needs of students and insufficient resources within the school, many principals reach outside the school walls, advocating for more support from social service agencies and law enforcement. Some extend their work out into the broader community and establish strategic partnerships with families, police, and other organizations. Of course, establishing and maintaining these partnerships requires a substantial investment of energy, which exacerbates the tasking time dilemma principals already must manage.

## STRATEGIES TO CREATE A SAFE SPACE

Principals can manage the dilemmas that arise as they work to create a safe space by helping teachers focus on the learning environment; cultivating a culture of all staff—themselves included—going above and beyond the call of duty; and building strategic partnerships.

## Help Students and Teachers Maintain a Focus on Learning

When he began his new position at Dogwood, Octavio recognized the particular challenges many of his students faced outside the school building. As recent immigrants with few resources and, in some cases, living without legal documentation, they were uncertain how long they or their families would be staying in the city. Acknowledging that there was little he could do to solve those problems, Octavio focused on what he could do to help Dogwood's students: "I need to make sure they have the learning environment they need—that their setting is safe, it's comfortable, and it is inviting," he said.

Octavio explained that he feels responsible for buffering teachers from intrusions and making sure they have what they need to teach effectively. This means focusing his attention on providing material resources, offering professional learning opportunities, and protecting teachers from classroom interruptions, which meant managing discipline issues or setting policy to ensure teaching time was sacred. Principals know they cannot tackle all the issues their students face, so they seek to fulfill their responsibility to students by helping them and their teachers focus on learning.

## Get All Hands on Deck

Creating and maintaining a safe and supportive learning environment is not easy and demands the creative use of all available resources. Working to establish a safe space for learning at Sweetgum, a brand-new school, Samantha needed all the support she could get from her staff. Her strategy was to assess the talent within the building and encourage everyone to contribute in as many ways as possible. As an example, she mentioned a bus aide with a college degree who trained with a literacy coach to learn how to use reading recovery strategies. Soon, the aide was spending the time between bus trips providing students with one-on-one literacy support. Samantha explained more about how her "all hands on deck" approach helped to establish Sweetgum's supportive, learning-focused culture:

Even if you're talking to one of the custodians, they know their job is important because they maintain the building where the kids come to learn. If the building is not clean or not safe, or if the kids can't stand the smell of something stinky, they're not going to learn. So that's just an example of how whatever role it is, it all is working toward having kids learn.

The "all hands on deck" strategy for creating a safe environment is built on the understanding that safety and learning are inextricably linked. Of course, at times staff need to do what it takes to care for students' safety first, which can entail doing things that may *not* appear to be directly linked to learning, such as providing snacks or addressing disruptive behaviors. For principals, this presents challenges for securing cooperation, as some staff may not be willing to go above and beyond, particularly when they don't see the relationship between additional duties and student learning. It can be a challenge to balance their efforts to buffer teachers from too many demands with the need for all hands to pitch in. Principals can manage this challenge by looking for hidden resources, highlighting how individual actions contribute to the whole, and ensuring that all staff share their commitment to fostering safe spaces for students.

## Develop Strategic Partnerships

Principals don't need to rely just on school staff when they take an "all hands on deck" approach; they can also seek out help from others. They often cope with the learning goal dilemma by supplementing an emphasis on academics with a focus on safety and well-being that allows for a rich and supportive learning environment. At Birch, Nelson and his staff were challenged to help students cope with instability, poverty, and trauma. Nelson discussed how he pursued grants that allowed Birch to partner with law enforcement and social services organizations. Critically, he strategically pursued certain partnerships over others, shaping his approach to meeting students' needs through the external resources he sought.

Relationships with community members offer opportunities to expand the boundaries of learning beyond the school walls. By setting up after-school opportunities with external organizations and partnering with various social service agencies to address socioemotional needs, principals can establish a range of partnerships to access additional resources that will directly and indirectly support learning. The strategy of identifying and pursuing outside partnerships with community-based resources is one that helps principals leverage assets within their communities to support the well-being of students within their schools.[3]

This is one way to manage the need for more support, but it also leads to dilemmas for principals as they strive to balance these bridging partnerships with their commitment to buffering teachers and students from external intrusions. Indeed, earlier in the book we described principals' efforts to establish boundaries between school and home and various other stakeholders. At the same time, these partnerships are resources that can promote physical safety, provide socioemotional support, or simply boost learning at home—all of which can support learning within the school building.

Note, too, that partnering with outside organizations adds to a principal's set of responsibilities. These organizations must be vetted, initial relationships must be built, and ongoing relationships must be maintained. This can make the tasking time dilemma all the more difficult to manage, as investing in these relationships diverts time and energy away from directly supporting teachers within the school. What's more, as principals create these bridges, they also increase the variety of stakeholders who may become demanding "squeaky wheels" and pull attention away from the day-to-day work in the building. Accordingly, principals must remain mindful of the benefits and limits of the partnerships and balance their own vision of leadership for their school with the value of bridging work among organizations. This means partnerships require ongoing attention, negotiation, and renegotiation to ensure that the focus remains on the needs of students and their learning, rather than the needs of partners. When navigating difficult decisions about when to buffer and when to bridge, principals benefit from keeping students at the heart of

---

[3] As Green (2017) illustrates in more detail, a systematic approach to learning about community-based resources can help principals develop a strategic set of partnerships on which to rely.

their decision making and centering the goal of fostering a safe school environment where students can thrive.

Managing the buffering and bridging dilemma means seeking to protect both students and teachers from outside factors that can disrupt learning, while making and sustaining connections that can ensure students and staff have security and resources that they need to foster and engage in productive learning. The work entails helping teachers maintain a focus on the classroom and balancing the learning goals dilemma of pursuing both academic and socioemotional growth by creating a culture where "all hands" are willing to contribute and building relationships with external partners. Despite the challenges facing the communities in which they work, principals use these strategies to work toward creating a safe space for their students and enrich learning both within and outside the school building.

## Discussion Questions

1. *Reflection:* Samantha's bridging efforts focused on helping parents learn to support their children's academic learning at home. However, she did not explore how she and her staff might have learned from students' parents and family members. What strategies might she have used to bring parent and family knowledge into the school?

2. *Application:* Partnerships with external organizations are not easy to maintain. Think of a partnership you or your school had that did not last. Why did it end? What might have been done differently to maintain it? What lessons can you draw from that experience about developing partnerships as school leaders?

3. *Implications:* Think of your school's community and demographic context (or imagine a context in which you might like to become the principal). What partnerships might you seek out to support your school? What untapped resources might be available in the community?

# A FINAL WORD

"I just think it fits me. I've always said that about teaching, and I think it's true about being a principal too. It's great, and I love it," Kathy said at the end of her fifth year as principal. At this point, she was no longer a novice and was well established in the same school where her principalship began. In an interview conducted a few months later, she added, "But you know, I think in some ways being a principal is kind of like being in a pot of boiling water."

In this telling juxtaposition, Kathy captured the meaning and intensity of the work of a principal. Among other conclusions we drew from the study was this: *principals love being principals.* Nothing else is like it, they say. They enjoy challenging work, opportunities to pursue their sense of social obligation on a daily basis, and working directly with children. Becoming a principal enabled them to do all these things on a grander scale than what was possible when they were teachers or in other administrative positions. The work rewards their aspirations.

At the same time, and often in the same breath, principals' love for the job is accompanied by a frank acknowledgment of the stress that it brings. Think of Kathy's "pot of boiling water" analogy or a similar one that Samantha offered at the end of her second year, when she said, "I have to take a break from the pressure cooker. That's what it feels like. You're always under the gun to produce, produce, produce—and you've got three people's jobs." She went on to note that the expectation to bring about change in short periods of time just adds to the feeling of being inside a pressure cooker.

## THE WORK–HOME DILEMMA

Constant stress is a reality of the principalship, yet principals persist. This is largely true of the principals in our study. Staying the course surfaces one more dilemma—that of balancing work life and home life. Like all dilemmas, the *work–home dilemma* is something principals must cope with and manage; it is not a problem that can be solved.

A few months into his principalship, Nathan was filled with passion for the work he was undertaking. "I'm loving it," he said. "I just think it's incredible. I mean it's nonstop, but it's so exciting!" Still, work–life balance was a concern for him from the start. He worried about "maintaining any resemblance of a good home. I mean, my wife is very supportive, but it's draining on her too." As a parent of three young children, including twins born during his first year on the job, Nathan struggled with this challenge. Even after two years on the job, he found it necessary to put in long hours, day and night. "I do all my e-mail—well, the vast majority of it—in the middle of the night. If the kids wake me up in the night, I can hit off 10 e-mails before I fall back asleep. I think my balance sucks, I really do," Nathan admitted. He shared concerns about his health and the health of his marriage, remarking on the many principals he knew who had gone through divorces owing to the toll of the job. Although he was relieved that his wife seemed to understand the demands of the principalship, he still worried about not striking the right balance.

This balance is not automatically achieved with time on the job. Kathy, after five years in the position, confessed that she continued to have trouble finding time for herself and her family. One advantage she had was that her own children attended Nyssa, which allowed her to see them during the day. But Kathy still found herself working late into the evening and on weekends. "It's almost 24/7, which isn't necessarily good for me," she said. "One of the things that I'm really trying to do is step back and focus on other aspects of my life." She went on to admit, "The night before last, I woke up at 2:30 in the morning, and I e-mailed myself a list of things that had to be done." For Kathy, as well as for others, the work–home dilemma is an ongoing challenge—a testament to the complex and never-ending demands of the principal position.

## WHAT HAPPENED TO THE STUDY PRINCIPALS?

After five or six years on the job, most of the principals in the study were still principals and still working in the same school where they started. Others had moved on to principal positions in different schools or had taken (or were eyeing) different educational leadership roles. One had returned to the classroom. Here is a snapshot of where each of the principals we profiled in this book was at the conclusion of the study:

- **Alejandro remained the principal at Hoptree,** which was taken off probation during his tenure. He credited the school's success to his investment in instruction and to the skill of his staff.
- **George was the principal at a rural school.** A few years into the study, he resigned as the principal of Buckthorn and relocated for family reasons. Reflecting back on his time at Buckthorn and his experiences at his new school, George expressed surprise at just how challenging it is to help teachers move away from deficit mindsets about students.
- **Janice remained the principal at Poplar.** She described being continually surprised by how multifaceted the work of a principal really is. Although she was pleased that she and her staff continued to move Poplar forward, she had started to consider her next step and begun training to become a superintendent.
- **Jennifer remained the principal at Bur Oak** and said that she couldn't imagine leaving the position. Toward the end of the study, she identified her biggest accomplishment as having built a team of teachers who work together to empower students and families.
- **Kathy remained the principal at Nyssa.** While she acknowledged that being a principal has its challenges, she explained, "If you enjoy it, the persisting is not that hard."
- **Nathan resigned his position as principal of Spruce.** Of all the principals in the study, he appeared to struggle most to balance his busy professional life with his responsibilities at home.
- **Nelson returned to the classroom** and continued to pursue his educational mission there. After his first year at Birch, the school was designated

for turnaround, and he assumed the principalship at a different school, also plagued by low performance. That school closed a few years later.

- **Octavio remained the principal at Dogwood.** Although he was not convinced that he will be a principal for the rest of his career, he remained focused on students and on being able "to provide for them the best of what we can do."

- **Oscar remained the principal at Tulip.** Though he recognized budgeting and strategic planning as significant challenges, Oscar's intrinsic desire for personal growth and a commitment to serve the Hispanic community led him to continue his work "for the foreseeable future."

- **Rich left the principalship, but not education.** Three years into this tenure at Sevenson, he was asked to assume leadership at a local education nonprofit. Rich expressed regret at not having achieved everything he wanted to at Sevenson, but he still described his time there as successful, singling out his efforts to encourage staff to take risks and try new approaches.

- **Samantha also left the principalship, and also remained in education.** After five years at Sweetgum, she took a leadership position in an education nonprofit, describing it as another means of "enhancing kids' lives in a real, deep, meaningful way." She looked back on her time as a principal as a success and viewed her current position as another step along the same path of motivating and inspiring youth.

## MOVING FORWARD WITH REALISM *AND* OPTIMISM

It's natural to want unequivocally happy endings and heroic accounts of principals successfully transforming schools and even the surrounding neighborhoods. New and aspiring principals may want to hear about Alejandro driving the gangs out of his neighborhood, or Samantha leading a crusade to clean up the air in hers. Some might settle for more modest acts of heroism: Nelson managing to double the number of students proficient in reading in just a few years, or Jennifer helping families support their children's summer learning.

There is no shortage of stories with such unequivocal happy ends in U.S. education. They deserve telling and deserve to be heard.

But those are not the stories we have—and to present them as such would be dishonest to the men and women in the principal's office who shared their insights with us over five or six years. It would also be dishonest to you who aspire to or are entering the principal position. In this book, our intention was to capture the complexity of the work of principals, from definitively solving problems to—as is most often the reality—effectively managing dilemmas.

Ultimately, we left this project with a sense of optimism, as most principals persist in their positions and persist with their own sense of optimism. Almost 90 percent of the 35 principals in our study were still principals five or six years on, and over 60 percent were principals in the school where they entered the principalship. They "made it" as principals, and they managed to do so by managing dilemmas that are part and parcel of becoming and being a principal.

# APPENDIX: STUDY METHODS

Data for this book come from a research project based at Northwestern University's School of Education and Social Policy and funded by the Spencer Foundation.

The primary goal of the research was to examine the transition and on-the-job socialization of new principals. To do so, researchers used a longitudinal, mixed-methods design, following two cohorts of new principals in the Chicago Public Schools for the first five to six years of their principalship. Cohort 1 began their principalships roughly a decade into the 21st century, and Cohort 2 began one year later.

Extensive data were gathered using multiple approaches including surveys, semi-structured interviews, administrative records, observations, and public documents. A subsample—a purposeful sample for Cohort 1 ($n = 18$) and randomly sampled for Cohort 2 ($n = 17$)—based on survey responses from the entire cohort were interviewed at regular intervals for five or more times over their first five or six years on the job, depending on the cohort (see Figure 2).

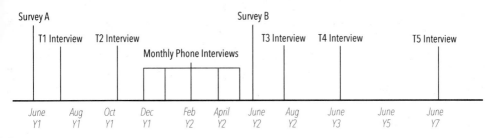

**Figure 2.** Data Collection Timeline

Key: T = Time, Y = Year

Principals were interviewed using semi-structured protocols immediately before starting their first school year as principal (Time 1), three months into that school year (Time 2), at the end of their first year on the job (Time 3), at the end of their second year on the job (Time 4), and, depending on the cohort, at the end of their fifth or sixth year on the job (Time 5). Each interview lasted between 45 and 90 minutes and was transcribed. Both inductive and deductive approaches were used to analyze the data using NVivo 8.

# REFERENCES

Ball, S. J. (2003). The teacher's soul and the terrors of performativity. *Journal of Education Policy, 18*(2), 215–228.

Coburn, C. E. (2006). Framing the problem of reading instruction: Using frame analysis to uncover the microprocesses of policy implementation. *American Educational Research Journal, 43*(3), 343–349.

Cohen, D. K. (2011). *Teaching and its predicaments.* Cambridge, MA: Harvard University Press.

Cuban, L. (1988). *The managerial imperative and the practice of leadership in schools.* Albany, NY: SUNY Press.

Cuban, L. (2001). *How can I fix it? Finding solutions and managing dilemmas: An educator's road map.* New York: Teachers College Press.

Delpit, L. (2006). *Other people's children: Cultural conflict in the classroom.* New York: New Press.

Epstein, J. L., Sanders, M. G., Sheldon, S. B., Simon, B. S., Salinas, K. C., Jansorn, N. R., . . . & Hutchins, D. J. (2018). *School, family, and community partnerships: Your handbook for action.* Thousand Oaks, CA: Corwin.

Galindo, C., Sanders, M., & Abel, Y. (2017). Transforming educational experiences in low-income communities: A qualitative case study of social capital in a full-service community school. *American Educational Research Journal, 54*(1suppl.), 140S–163S.

Goodlad, J. I. (1990). *Teachers for our nation's schools*. San Francisco: Jossey-Bass.

Green, T. L. (2017). Community-based equity audits: A practical approach for educational leaders to support equitable community-school improvements. *Educational Administration Quarterly, 53*(1), 3–39.

Ladson-Billings, G. (2009). *The dreamkeepers: Successful teachers of African American children* (2nd ed.). Hoboken, NJ: Wiley.

Lampert, M. (1985). How do teachers manage to teach? Perspectives on problems in practice. *Harvard Educational Review, 55*(2), 178–195.

Lee, L. C. (2015). School performance trajectories and the challenges for principal succession. *Journal of Educational Administration, 53*(2), 262–286.

Lipsky, M. (2010). *Street-level bureaucracy* (30th ann. ed.). *Dilemmas of the individual in public service*. New York: Russell Sage Foundation.

Lortie, D. (1975). *Schoolteacher: A sociological analysis*. Chicago: University of Chicago Press.

Majone, G. (1989). *Evidence, argument, and persuasion in the policy process*. New Haven, CT: Yale University Press.

Mehta, J. (2013). How paradigms create politics: The transformation of American educational policy, 1980–2001. *American Educational Research Journal, 50*(2), 285–324.

Moll, L. C., Amanti, C., Neff, D., & Gonzalez, N. (1992). Funds of knowledge for teaching: Using a qualitative approach to connect homes and classrooms. *Theory into Practice, 31*(2), 132–141.

Moore, M. H. (1976). Anatomy of the heroin problem: An exercise in problem definition. *Policy Analysis, 2*(4), 639–662.

Orfield, G., Ee, J., Frankenberg, E., & Siegel-Hawley, G. (2016). Brown *at 62: School segregation by race, poverty and state*. Los Angeles: Civil Rights Project/Proyecto Derechos Civiles.

Prado Tuma, A., & Spillane, J. P. (2019). Novice school principals constructing their role vis-à-vis external stakeholders: (Not) attempting to be "all things to all people." *Educational Administration Quarterly*. Retrieved from https://journals.sagepub.com/doi/10.1177/0013161X 18822101

Spillane, J. P. (2009). *Standards deviation: How schools misunderstand education policy*. Cambridge, MA: Harvard University Press.

Spillane, J. P., & Anderson, L. (2014). The architecture of anticipation and novices' emerging understandings of the principal position: Occupational sense making at the intersection of individual, organization, and institution. *Teachers College Record, 116*(7), 1–42.

Spillane, J. P., & Lee, L. C. (2014). Novice school principals' sense of ultimate responsibility: Problems of practice in transitioning to the principal's office. *Educational Administration Quarterly, 50*(3), 431–465.

Suárez-Orozco, M., & Páez, M. (2002). *Latinos: Remaking America*. Berkeley, CA: University of California Press.

Tschannen-Moran, M. (2014). *Trust matters*. San Francisco: Jossey-Bass.

Valencia, R. R. (2010). *Dismantling contemporary deficit thinking: Educational thought and practice*. New York: Routledge.

# INDEX

The letter *f* following a page locator denotes a figure.

apprenticeships, formal and informal, 23–25

buffering and bridging dilemma, 97, 99–101, 104, 106, 109

center children strategy, 45–47
commitment and control dilemma, 70–71
commitment strategy, 68–69
competition for students, 8
consistency dilemma, 42–43
control strategy, 69–70
cooperation and coordination
   coordination, pursuing, 73–75
   coordination challenges, 75–77
   diagnostic work and challenges of, 64–67
   egalitarian dilemma, 71
   importance of, 63–64
   urgency for results dilemma, 78

cooperation and coordination, design work for
   challenges of, 67
   commitment and control dilemma, 70–71
   commitment strategy for cooperation, 68–69
   control strategy for cooperation, 69–70
   skills development, 71–73
cooperation and coordination management strategies
   build infrastructure, 78–79
   coax others along, 77–78
   differentiate approaches, 79
   involve staff, 77–78
   summary overview, 80
crossings, inside and outside
   navigating, 13–15
   tasks and time management, 53–54

decisionism, 12
decision making, sharing, 34–35

delegate with oversight, 33–34, 57
dilemmas, managing, 9–12
diplomacy dilemma, 41–42

egalitarian dilemma, 01, 71, 82,
    87–88

grease the squeaky wheel, 47–48

infrastructure, building, 78
instruction–management balance,
    31–33

leadership, modeling, 4–5
leadership shared
    benefits of, 82–83
    compromise in, 90
    egalitarian dilemma, 82
    investing in staff for, 83–85
    leveraging, 92
    reasons for, 81–82
    responsibility dilemma, 82,
        83–84
    scaffolding, 93–94
    summary overview, 95
leadership shared, challenges of
    egalitarian dilemma, 01,
        87–88
    favoritism, perceptions of,
        87–88
    managing expectations, 91
    responsibility dilemma,
        86–87
    time and money, 90
    trust, building and
        maintaining, 88–90

leadership shared, strategies
    supporting
        allies, identify and enlist, 91–92
        gradual release of control,
            93–95
        placement, right people, right
            roles, 92–93
leadership teams, 87–88, 90, 92–93
learning goal dilemma, 101

mindset adjustment, 34–35

norms, setting and modeling, 34–35

parent partnerships, 101–104
parent stakeholders, 40–42, 44–45,
    47–48
performance metrics, 6–7, 11
performativity, 12
personal fulfillment as a motivator,
    2–3
policy churn, 8–9
poverty, challenge of, 9
principals
    assistant, 24–26
    backgrounds of, 1, 13
    challenges for, 2–4, 6–9
    dilemmas, managing, 9–12
    expectations for, 26–27
    motivators, 2–6
    navigating different crossings,
        13–17
    profiled, 18f–21f, 113–115
    roles played by, 58, 64
    work–home dilemma, 52–55,
        60, 112

principalship
    love of, 111
    stress of, 55, 111
    study methods, 116–117
problems, defining and solving, 10–12. *See also* dilemmas, managing

responsibilities
    balancing, 52–55, 60, 109, 112
    familiar, 23–26
    new, more, and different, 26–27
    summary overview, 35–36
    task-time management and, 56–58
    ultimate, 27–30, 56–57, 60–61
responsibilities, managing
    delegate with oversight, 33–34, 57
    managerial and instructional balance, 31–33
    share decision making, 28, 34–35
responsibility dilemma, 82, 83–84, 86–87

safe spaces
    buffering and bridging dilemma, 97, 99–101, 104, 106, 109
    buffering from outside forces, 97–99
    community in, 97–98
    defining, 97
    learning goal dilemma, 101

safe spaces (*continued*)
    outside of school, 100
    parents, partnering with, 101–104
    prioritizing, 96–97, 98–99
    safety nets and, 98–99
    summary overview, 110
    support from outside sources, 104–107
safe spaces, strategies to create
    all hands on deck approach, 107–108
    focus on learning, 107
    strategic partnerships, 108–110
schools, competition for students, 8
skills development, 78
social obligation motivator, 3–6, 56
squeaky wheel, grease the, 47–48
staff
    creating safe spaces, 110
    empowering, 83–84, 88–89, 92–93
    involving for cooperation/coordination, 78
stakeholder challenges
    conflicting and competing demands, 29, 44–45
    consistency dilemma, 42–43
    diplomacy dilemma, 41–42
    expectations, managing, 37–38
    summary overview, 50
    transparency dilemma, 43–44

stakeholder challenges, managing
    center children, 45–47
    grease the squeaky wheel,
        47–48
    reconsider the principal's role,
        48–49
stakeholders
    buffering and bridging
        dilemma, 97
    crucial, 40
    expectations of, 38–41
    external, 39–41
    internal, 38–39
    meeting the needs of all, 37
    responsibility to, 37
    task-time management and,
        56–58
students, competition for, 8
success, stakeholders' role in, 38–39

tasking time dilemma, 51–52
task-time management
    external crossings, influence of,
        53–54
    internal crossings, influence of,
        53–54
    learning curve, 54–56
    perpetual need for, 55–56
    tasking time dilemma, 51–52

task-time management challenges
    obligation, responsibility,
        stakeholders, 56–58
    obligations, 56–58
    responsibilities, 56–58
    stakeholders, 56–58
    task diversity, 58–59
    unpredictability of the work,
        58–59
    work–home dilemma, 52–55,
        60
task-time management strategies
    boundaries, establishing, 60
    embrace the challenge,
        61–62
    prioritize tasks, 59
    protect specific times, 60–61
    savor the rush, 61–62
    summary overview, 62
transparency dilemma, 43–44
trust, building and maintaining,
    88–90

urgency for results dilemma, 78

wicked problems, 10–11
work–home dilemma, 52–55, 60,
    112

# ABOUT THE AUTHORS

**James P. Spillane** is the Spencer T. and Ann W. Olin Professor in Learning and Organizational Change at the School of Education and Social Policy at Northwestern University. He is also professor of Human Development and Social Policy, professor of Learning Sciences, professor (by courtesy) of Management and Organizations, and faculty associate at Northwestern's Institute for Policy Research. Spillane has published extensively on issues of education policy, policy implementation, school reform, and school leadership. His work explores the policy implementation process at the state, district, school, and classroom levels, focusing on intergovernmental and policy–practice relations. He also studies organizational leadership and change, conceptualizing organizational leadership as a distributed practice.

Spillane's recent projects include studies of relations between organizational infrastructure and instructional advice seeking in schools and the socialization of new school principals. His work has been supported by the National Science Foundation, Institute of Education Sciences, Spencer Foundation, Sherwood Foundation, and Carnegie Corporation of New York. He has authored several books, including *Standards Deviation: How Local Schools Misunderstand Policy* (Harvard University Press, 2004), *Distributed Leadership* (Jossey-Bass, 2006), *Distributed Leadership in Practice* (Teachers College Press, 2011), and *Diagnosis and Design for School Improvement* (Teachers College Press,

2011), and has contributed numerous journal articles and book chapters. In 2013, he was awarded the Ver Steeg Research Fellowship at Northwestern University and was also elected to the National Academy of Education.

**Rebecca Lowenhaupt** is an associate professor of Educational and Higher Leadership at Boston College's Lynch School of Education and Human Development. She studies the role that school principals—and other school and district leaders—play in supporting culturally diverse students. Drawing on multiple methods of empirical research, including survey methods, social network analysis, and qualitative analysis, her work investigates educational leadership and policy in the context of immigration, with a focus on new immigrant destinations. At Boston College, she teaches aspiring school and district leaders about teacher supervision, organizational theory, and research methods.

A former middle school English teacher, she received her bachelor's and master's degrees from Harvard University and earned her doctoral degree from the University of Wisconsin, Madison. Lowenhaupt has received funding for her work from the Spencer Foundation, W. T. Grant Foundation, and National Science Foundation. She serves as an associate editor for the journal *Educational Policy* and has contributed to numerous scholarly articles and book chapters. You may contact her at rebecca.lowenhaupt@bc.edu and follow her on Twitter @RLowenhaupt.

## Related ASCD Resources: The Principalship

At the time of publication, the following resources were available (ASCD stock numbers in parentheses):

**PD Online® Courses**
Leadership: Effective Critical Skills (#PD09OC08M)
What Works in Schools: School Leadership in Action, 2nd ed. (#PD11OC119M)

**Print Products**
*The Aspiring Principal 50: Critical Questions for New and Future School Leaders*
    by Baruti K. Kafele (#112023)
*The Coach Approach to School Leadership: Leading Teachers to Higher Levels of*
    *Effectiveness* by Jessica Johnson, Shira Leibowitz, and Kathy Perret (#117025)
*Improving Student Learning One Principal at a Time* by Jane E. Pollock and
    Sharon M. Ford (#109006)
*Leading in Sync: Teacher Leaders and Principals Working Together for Student*
    *Learning* by Jill Harrison Berg (#118021)
*Never Underestimate Your Teachers: Instructional Leadership for Excellence in Every*
    *Classroom* by Robyn R. Jackson (#110028)
*Principal Evaluation: Standards, Rubrics, and Tools for Effective Performance*
    by James H. Stronge, Xianxuan Xu, Lauri Leeper, and Virginia Tonneson
    (#113025)
*The Principal Influence: A Framework for Developing Leadership Capacity in*
    *Principals* by Pete Hall, Deborah Childs-Bowen, Ann Cunningham-Morris,
    Phyllis Pajardo, and Alisa Simeral (#116026)
*Qualities of Effective Principals* by James H. Strong, Holly B. Richard, and Nancy
    Catano (#108003)
*You're the Principal! Now What? Strategies and Solutions for New School Leaders*
    by Jen Schwanke (#117003)

For up-to-date information about ASCD resources, go to www.ascd.org. You can search the complete archives of *Educational Leadership* at www.ascd.org/el.

For more information, send an e-mail to member@ascd.org; call 1-800-933-2723 or 703-578-9600; send a fax to 703-575-5400; or write to Information Services, ASCD, 1703 N. Beauregard St., Alexandria, VA 22311-1714 USA.

# WHOLE CHILD
# TENETS

The ASCD Whole Child approach is an effort to transition from a focus on narrowly defined academic achievement to one that promotes the long-term development and success of all children. Through this approach, ASCD supports educators, families, community members, and policymakers as they move from a vision about educating the whole child to sustainable, collaborative actions.

*Navigating the Principalship* relates to the **healthy, safe, supported,** and **challenged** tenets.
*For more about the ASCD Whole Child approach, visit* **www.ascd.org/wholechild.**

### 1 HEALTHY
Each student enters school healthy and learns about and practices a healthy lifestyle.

### 2 SAFE
Each student learns in an environment that is physically and emotionally safe for students and adults.

### 3 ENGAGED
Each student is actively engaged in learning and is connected to the school and broader community.

### 4 SUPPORTED
Each student has access to personalized learning and is supported by qualified, caring adults.

### 5 CHALLENGED
Each student is challenged academically and prepared for success in college or further study and for employment and participation in a global environment.

LEARN. TEACH. LEAD.